JOE AND MUZ IBACH, LEMESURIER ISLAND, 1954

Copyright Bruce Black. Courtesy of Dave Bohn.

BOOK ONE OF THE SEQUENCE

IF A PLACE COULD SPEAK

EVERYTHING THEY WANTED
MUZ AND JOE, REID INLET, AND GLACIER BAY

JUDITH B. AFTERGUT

GOOSE COVE PRESS, BERKELEY
PUBLICATION #8

Book One of the Sequence
If A Place Could Speak

Everything They Wanted:
Muz and Joe, Reid Inlet, and Glacier Bay

Goose Cove Press, Berkeley

Printed by CreateSpace 2015
Copyright © 2015 Judith B. Aftergut

All rights reserved. No part of this publication may be reproduced, distributed, or transmitted in any form or by any means, including photocopying, recording, or other electronic or mechanical methods, without the prior written permission of the publisher, except in the case of brief quotations embodied in critical reviews and certain other noncommercial uses permitted by copyright law. For permission requests, contact the publisher.

ISBN 978-0-692-50457-4 Paperback

Library of Congress Catalogue Control Number 2015915177

Cover photo of Reid Glacier © 2006 Fritz Koschmann
Artwork by Carole Baker © 1996-2013 Carole Baker

Designed by Leia Reedijk.

We appreciate direct orders from the publisher.
orders@goosecovepress.com
www.goosecovepress.com

Printed in the United States of America.

For SWZ
and for DSM

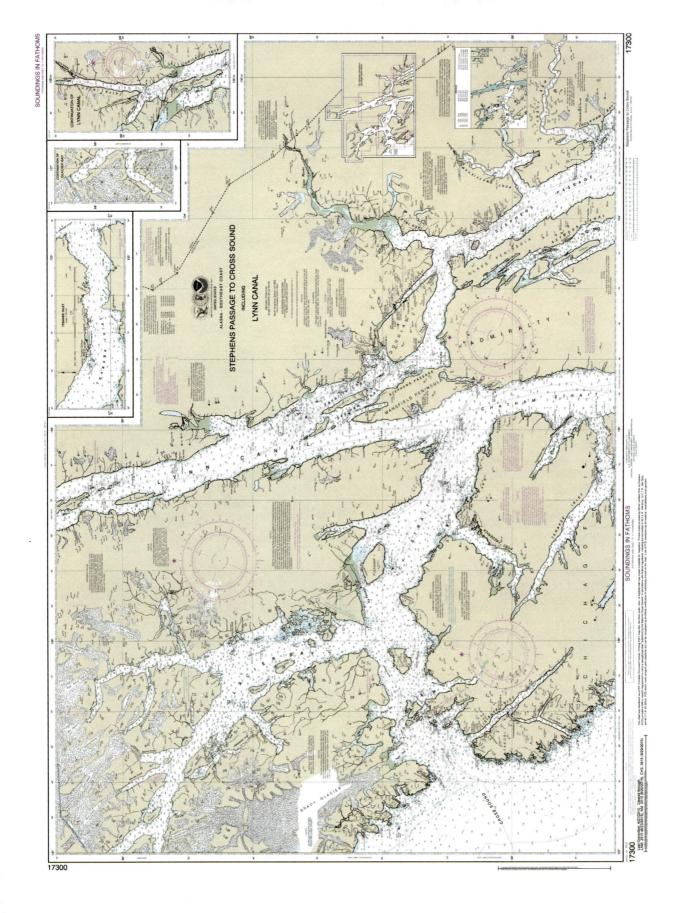

IF A PLACE COULD SPEAK

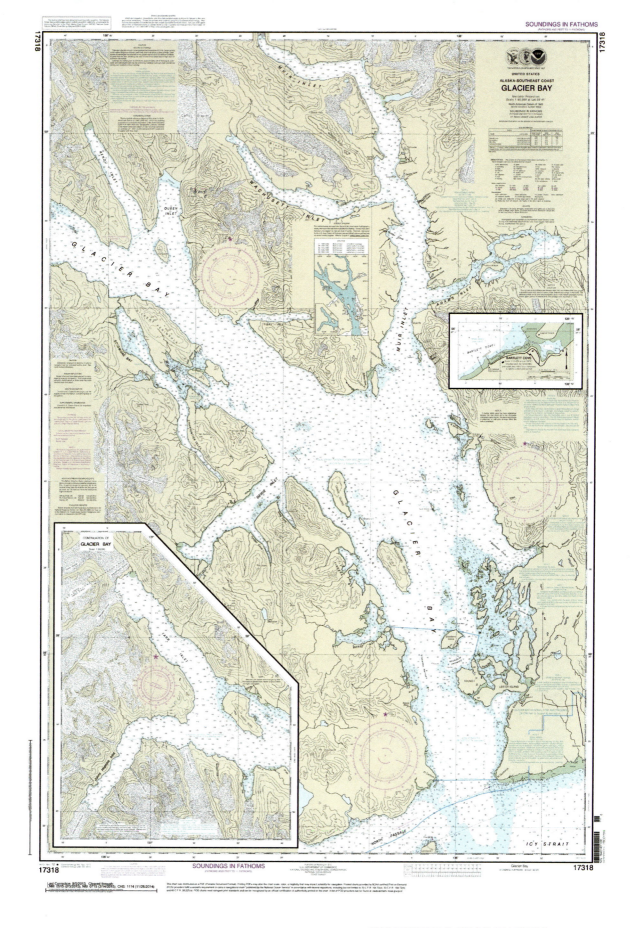

We are fifteen hundred feet above the cabins and looking north to Tarr Inlet...This is the vantage point from which I see everything that is Glacier Bay...Two years ago there was silence, and tonight there is silence. But the sound lingers on when one has heard. Down the centuries the booming primeval thunder.

Dave Bohn, *Glacier Bay: The Land and the Silence*

FIREWEED MEADOW, GUSTAVUS, WATERCOLOR, 1996

Copyright Carole Baker.

VIEW FROM JON AND CAROLYN'S, GUSTAVUS, WATERCOLOR, 1996

Copyright Carole Baker.

THE CHILD AND THE FISH

The child still has gills.
The water is salmon and silver, reflecting sky.
My child is a fetus,
an image with curls black as your sweater,
who never will swim up the river to spawn.

SALMON RIVER BRIDGE NO. I, GUSTAVUS, WATERCOLOR, 1996

Copyright Carole Baker.

VIEW FROM THE SMOKEHOUSE WITH THE SALMON RIVER, PLEASANT ISLAND, AND ICY STRAIT IN THE BACKGROUND, WATERCOLOR, 1996

Copyright Carole Baker.

CONTENTS

Epigraph ix
The Child and the Fish xi
Contents .... xiii - xiv
List of Images .... xv - xvii
Preface to the Sequence: If A Place Could Speak .... xix - xxii
Prelude: Everything They Wanted xxiii
Place Names xxv

Muz and Joe .... 3 - 4
Questions .... 5 - 6
Summer 1974 .... 7 - 11
Ice Country .... 13 - 16
Migration .... 17 - 18
Learning to Kayak .... 19 - 20
Becoming a Writer .... 21 - 24
The Ibachs' Cabin .... 25 - 28
Moment in Time .... 29 - 30
Mining .... 33 - 34
Suicide Pact 35
Nell Parker .... 37 - 41
Mound of Pansies .... 47 - 50
Ken Youmans .... 53 - 55
Following the Trail .... 57 - 58
Scabies .... 59 - 62
George Shurin 63
Radio Waves .... 65 - 66

Mike Seiler	69 - 77
Transformation	79 - 82
Doc G	83 - 87
The Cairn	89 - 91
Friends	93 - 94
Becoming an Ibach	97 - 100
Reid Inlet Return	101 - 105
Leslie Parker	107
What She Wanted	109 - 114
Fog	115 - 118
Afterword	121
Acknowledgements	123 - 125
Bibliography	126

LIST OF IMAGES

Joe and Muz Ibach, Lemesurier Island, 1954, *Bruce Black* ii

Map of Alaska, Southeast Coast, Stephens Passage to Cross Sound, including Lynn Canal (showing Glacier Bay, Reid Inlet, and Lemesurier Island), No. 17300, *Courtesy of the National Oceanic and Atmospheric Administration* vi

Map of Alaska, Southeast Coast, Glacier Bay, No. 17318, *Courtesy of the National Oceanic and Atmospheric Administration* vii

Fireweed Meadow, Watercolor, 1996, *Carole Baker* x

View from Jon and Carolyn's, Watercolor, 1996, *Carole Baker* x

Salmon River Bridge No. 1, Gustavus, Watercolor, 1996, *Carole Baker* xii

View from the Smokehouse with the Salmon River, Pleasant Island, and Icy Strait in the Background, Watercolor, 1996, *Carole Baker* xii

Lamplugh Glacier, Watercolor, 2011, *Carole Baker* xviii

Point Adolphus, Gouache, 2013, *Carole Baker* xxiv

The Ibach Cabin Group: the Blacksmith Hut, the Salmon Trap Cabin, and the Ibach Cabin, Reid Inlet, Mid-Summer 1966, *Dave Bohn* 2

Cold Mountain Morning: Gustavus Beach and the Fairweather Range, 2011, *Fritz Koschmann* 8

Brown Bears, Reid Inlet, 2007, *Fritz Koschmann* 12

Reid Glacier Dwarfing Visitors, 2006, *Fritz Koschmann* 22

Reid Glacier and the Ibach Cabin Group Series, 1985, *Robert E. Howe* 26

Bedroom: Inside the Ibachs' Cabin, Reid Inlet, May 1969, *Dave Bohn* 31

Reid Glacier and the Sea, 2006, *Fritz Koschmann* 32

Mrs. Wade (Missionary) and Nell Crowell Visiting Southeast Alaska, Summer 1937, *Courtesy of Gustavus Historical Archives and Antiquities* 36

Gathering Hay on the Gustavus Beach in Les Parker's Truck Near the Site of the Present-Day Dock, 1937, *Courtesy of Gustavus Historical Archives and Antiquities* 42

Glen Parker Alongside His First Ditch, Looking North From the Gustavus Beach Towards the Beartrack Mountains, 1930s, *Courtesy of Gustavus Historical Archives and Antiquities* 43

Wedding Day of Nell Crowell and Glen Parker at the Home of Edith A. and Abraham Lincoln Parker, Gustavus, June 10, 1938, *Courtesy of Gustavus Historical Archives and Antiquities* 44

Joe and Muz Ibach with Glen Parker, Lemesurier Island, 1940s, *Courtesy of Gustavus Historical Archives and Antiquities* 45

Joe Ibach, Reid Inlet, August 18, 1936, *John C. Reed, Sr., U.S. Geological Survey* 46

Ibach Headstone, Willoughby Cove, Lemesurier Island, April 1999, *Dave Bohn* 51

Ken Youmans and Joe Ibach, Lemesurier Island, October 1954, *Bruce Black* 52

Ken Youmans, 1989, *Jim Mackovjak* 56

Sea Lions, Point Carolus, 2006, *Fritz Koschmann* 64

Letter from Joe Ibach to Jack and Shirley Callahan, June 1, 1959, *Courtesy of John D. Feagin, Sr.* 67

William O. Field and Dave Bohn, Hugh Miller Inlet, September 1966, *Lynn Kinsman* 68

Dryas Seeds, 2004, *Sean Neilson* 78

Barbara Washburn Descending First Few Steps of Mount Bertha, Glacier Bay National Monument, Alaska, 1940, *Bradford Washburn* 84

Gravel Waterfall, Upper Muir Inlet, 1980, *Fritz Koschmann* 88

Kate Boesser, Gustavus, 1995, *Courtesy of Kate Boesser* 92

Dark Ice at Reid Glacier, 2011, *Fritz Koschmann* 95

Descendancy Chart of Josef Ibach 96

Flowers at Reid Inlet: *Dryas* and Indian Paintbrush, Watercolor, 2012, *Carole Baker* 102

Mike Seiler, Viola the Camp Cook, and Les Parker, Leroy Mine, Ptarmigan Creek, circa 1942, *Courtesy of Gustavus Historical Archives and Antiquities* 106

Ibach Cabin Cradled by Alders, Reid Inlet, 2007, *Kate Boesser* 108

The *Great Sea* in Fog, 2006, *Carole Baker* 116

Entrance to Reid Inlet, February 1968, *Dave Bohn* 118

Reid Glacier and *Dryas* Field, 2004, *Sean Neilson* 120

LAMPLUGH GLACIER, WATERCOLOR, 2011

Copyright Carole Baker.

PREFACE TO THE SEQUENCE: IF A PLACE COULD SPEAK

The books in this series are memoir. Their theme is being. As a writer, I say: read them as the evolution of a perspective, a way of seeing the world, a way of thinking. I meant them to be this way. I wrote them this way on purpose.

These books contain both extroverted and introverted worlds, as did my life growing up. They include emotions. Their original focus was the years between 1974 and 1981, a brief speck of time in the history of Glacier Bay, with background from the years before and awareness from the years after.

They began as oral history interviews, gathering information and then stepping back, but they have a more related style than history in the usual sense. One theme is how a person can meet the people in these stories and the issues they deal with spirit-to-spirit—as Gertrude Stein, in a completely different place, wanted readers to do with the characters she described. In my early Glacier Bay years, when I saw the world in terms of a masculine/feminine divide, the feminine side had relationships spirit-to-spirit and explored ideas in a non-linear way. This method of relating is a feminist issue in the best sense of the word, says Megan Brown, my editor. Megan, a teacher of logic, should know, for logic involves the recognition of people's philosophies and assumptions. To relate spirit-to-spirit is to see a person's true beauty within, no matter how they appear.

Dave Bohn, the author of *Glacier Bay: The Land and the Silence*, had an idea: hold a lottery offering access to Glacier Bay. The Park Service would draw lots from a pool of names. Allow one, two or three people to go into the bay alone for a few days, a week or a month in a kayak or skiff. Keep everyone else out. See what a person who went alone up the bay came back with. What could they tell the rest of us? What did they see? That way, he thought, changes in the lands and waters of the bay would occur according to the natural process, and collectively we would gain the kind of wisdom that might come to a person who spent time alone there.

Bohn spent forty nights up there in a tent in the 1960s, keeping a journal and taking photographs, so he had the kind of credibility that counts. Many Alaskans would disagree with Dave's idea, including, perhaps, Tlingit people whose sacred land this is, but no one, not even the superintendent, has the power to manage Glacier Bay National Park like that.

I took on Dave's assignment in secret, winning a lottery that never was announced. No one else knew it existed, so I didn't have much competition. I didn't spend a summer, or even a week, alone up in Glacier Bay. One night at a time alone was my limit. But I studied the shape of that land as if it would provide the answer to a mystery. For thirty years I read and re-read transcripts of interviews I'd recorded in the late years of the seventh decade of the twentieth century—women and men, homesteaders and scientists, park managers and fishermen, anyone who would speak to me.

I sought to find, through the words and phrases they used, the reality within—an access to the mystic and the eternal—in the same way any Jew trained in *Torah* would deeply study the stories of the *Five Books of Moses* and seek meaning to understand her life. I didn't tell anyone I was doing this, including Dave Bohn, but the interviews seemed like a promise to those people that their stories would be told. It's a promise I intend to honor.

In 1976, at a loss about how to write about Glacier Bay, I first met Dave in the old Park Service office building next to the lagoon in Bartlett Cove. He listened to my quandary and suggested writing a book about what people can learn from a place where they witness the process of change before their eyes in brief increments. He nurtured the concept and my own sense of myself as a writer until I could stand on my own two feet. The books have changed form since then. One long book has morphed into five smaller ones, or however many it turns out to be, but Dave Bohn was right on track. In every place that exists, one thing arises and another disappears, but there is much to learn in a place where these changes are obvious: one change to grieve and another to celebrate.

My belief is that people are characters, and I want to know more about them, my editor says.

I believe we are shaped by landscapes.
I believe we are shaped by stories.
I believe that the stories we hear affect us across lines of culture.

I believe that the people who know a place well have things to teach. In this series of books I seek both what's on the surface and what might be hidden beneath it. Perhaps I do this because I knew there was a subterranean aspect of my mother, who had her own personal agendas as well as a hidden, clear soul.

The people I write of are not perfect. I take the liberty of finding the best in them. The modern message I offer is not about saving the planet or the Jewish idea of repairing the world (*tikkun olam*). The message here is that anything—a person, a glacier, or a rock—may form itself into a shape temporarily, and that's not all it is. Loss and grief are, then, inevitable, if we're willing to be open.

As an inquirer, a questioner, I love the language of science and the challenge of trying to learn what it means and to say that in simpler words. Listening to people deeply is required to translate from science to ordinary language. I honor what scientists do. I think there's a way to do science and remain present to the mystery all around us, the mystery with which we are connected and in which we live.

Manifestations are aspects of a whole. They take a particular form for a time. Any concrete manifestation is temporary, one form of wholeness complete in itself, yet also shifting and changing.

One example of this assertion: in English we can never say a whole idea at once. We say phrases one after another. We can never describe our whole selves in any moment. The whole world is like that, says my editor Megan. You can walk and talk at the same time, but many things you can't do all at once. You can't, for instance, take a bath and iron a shirt. Even a shape is temporary: the legs of a wooden table can fall off, and they can burn in a fire. The table's structure breaks down; the wood turns to ash. Our eyes see objects as solid, but so much space exists between atomic particles that it's a wonder that a stone, a drop of water, an oystercatcher, or anything at all holds together.

It is possible, Megan says, to write a book that is whole even when you are making the statement in it that no manifestation of anything is all of what it is. Doing this, she asserts, takes a certain kind of intelligence. It's a paradox in style.

Fixed, unchanging and solid are concepts, illusions. We come from the earth and dissolve back into it. This idea may scare some people. At times it scares me, too. My purpose is to honor the idea that nothing is truly solid or unchanging. This belief/this fact is fundamental to everything I've written here.

Glacier Bay speaks in the sound of the wind blowing through the branches of spruce and hemlock trees, in the sounds of the waves, of rivers and streams, in the underwater songs of whales. The words of the people who know a place also become its voice.

These books draw no conclusions. They record a few frozen moments, a series of crystalline fragments. They reflect an inquiry over forty years, a brief time in glaciated land. I don't know what has happened to all of the people I interviewed years ago, although I know for some. The single life continuously referenced in this series of books is mine.

From my perspective, to honor is to choose the highest and best action (including no action) that I can see in any situation. Since these books are meant to honor a place and its people, I haven't always used real names. I have referenced but not told the sacred Tlingit story of how the ice came down into Glacier Bay. At one point I thought it would honor Tlingit people to tell their story, but in this I was mistaken, although their story has meant as much to me as any of the biblical stories I grew up with. I have chosen not to tell the Tlingit story because I don't have permission from the elders who are its owners and guardians. That story belongs to them. The related story of my own grief and reconnection to living in joy is mine to tell.

My story flows in and out of others' personal histories and weaves through the Tlingit story of why the ice came down into Glacier Bay like a braided outwash river.

PRELUDE: EVERYTHING THEY WANTED

"Five thousand years ago, Glacier Bay was a river valley," I read in Dave Bohn's book *Glacier Bay: The Land and the Silence*. I first heard that number, five thousand years, in Sunday school when I was six. I linked it with the history of the Jewish people I came from and to the holiness of land. I grew up in a land of two rivers, the Mississippi and the Missouri. The idea of five thousand years was familiar, although Southeast Alaska was not. My first summer in Glacier Bay was 1974, the year 5734 in the Hebrew calendar.

I believe that land is holy. I believe that stories are sacred. I believe that one way to wisdom is by telling the experiences of our lives and the stories we inherit and by exploring them with other people. I came to these beliefs from listening to the *Torah* chanted on Sabbath mornings in a modern pale brick St. Louis synagogue, where old men who spoke Yiddish in daily life faced east toward Jerusalem to pray. They blessed the wine but preferred to drink schnapps. I watched as it dripped down their beards. I believe that places and the specific energies they hold shape our ideas and thought process: that a person can see the world differently by living in the Missouri hills or a rainforest or a desert than on the tall grass prairies or in a mangrove swamp.

"We are the land, and the land is us," Dave Bohn once said.

We accept that people and places change, but we often hold onto concepts, like the idea of one holy land, and we fight wars over places and ideas. I believe that every human being is holy and so is all of the land.

In Hebrew, the word *makom*, which means "place," is one of many words for God.

POINT ADOLPHUS,
GOUACHE, 2013
Copyright Carole Baker.

PLACE NAMES

In current lingo, the term "Glacier Bay" is used in several ways. It refers to a landscape, that is, to the bay itself: the "inside" waters, the two-pronged fjord, in contrast to the "outside waters" of the Pacific Ocean. It also refers to Glacier Bay as a legal entity.

The first form of that entity was Glacier Bay National Monument, created by President Calvin Coolidge on February 25, 1925. In 1939, President Franklin D. Roosevelt issued a proclamation that doubled the size of the monument. In 1955, some of the monument lands, including lands around the town of Gustavus and 10,000 acres at Excursion Inlet, were returned to public domain.

In 1980, Congress added land and designated Glacier Bay as a national park (3.3 million acres) and preserve (an additional 57,000 acres). The term "Glacier Bay" in that context refers to all the lands and waters of the park and preserve, extending north from Icy Strait, Cross Sound and Cape Spencer almost to Yakutat.

In these books, I use terminology the way it is used by people who live near this place. Going "up bay" means a trip north into Glacier Bay proper: the inside waters carved by ice into two great channels now called Muir Inlet and the West Arm. In contrast, going to the "outer coast" means a trip to the parklands along the open Pacific.

The name "Glacier Bay" is temporary. Glacier Bay didn't always exist. Tlingit people have three names for the bay, based upon different geologic conditions.

The current glaciers will disappear even if the name Glacier Bay remains.

EVERYTHING THEY WANTED

THE IBACH CABIN GROUP: THE BLACKSMITH HUT, THE SALMON TRAP CABIN, AND THE IBACH CABIN, REID INLET, MID-SUMMER 1966

Copyright Dave Bohn.

MUZ AND JOE

I fell in love with Muz and Joe Ibach, although they were both long dead. I read about them in Dave Bohn's book, that great Glacier Bay primer *Glacier Bay: The Land and the Silence*, the original version in hard cover, 10-1/4 inches by 14, with photographs so clear and real that I could almost fall into them.

I read Dave Bohn's book the way I read fairy tales as a child and listened to Bible stories. It provided history, philosophy, and tales of the Glacier Bay world I now lived in, stories of the scientists and homesteaders and people at the park with Dave's clear voice in the background. For me this book was sacred text.

I read Dave's book on early summer evenings as I lay on my bunk in the Lodge employee trailer my first year in Glacier Bay, after long days hauling laundry, cleaning toilets, and making beds, the hardest physical labor I'd ever done. Each night I fell asleep about nine o'clock, exhausted after cleaning rooms, although swallows were hunting mosquitoes near the dock and the sky would be light for hours. I alternated reading Dave Bohn's book and the fat paperback I had stuffed into my suitcase, Alexandr Solzhenitsyn's *The First Circle*. Southeast Alaska was far from Missouri, and I was nowhere near Siberia. Still, my mind connected housekeeping, its hard work, its low status and wages with the idea of prison camps and slave labor. Perhaps I sought freedom from hopelessness, depression and despair. (I didn't inherit my mother's bipolar chemistry but I had been living the low end of her pattern).

In the journal, I wrote after a week, "Last night I felt I was in prison. Bone weary, no fresh fruit or vegetables. My eyes were burning from the ammonia we used to clean. So tired I wanted to scream." But I also wrote, "Every movement is a slowing down. How quiet it is here."

Bohn wrote that Muz Ibach died in the hospital in Juneau in 1959, and Joe Ibach shot himself a year later. I wanted to know more about these two people who lived each summer in a cabin they built in that Glacier Bay wilderness and who loved one another so much that they couldn't imagine living without each other.

4

Bohn's book contains a photograph of Joe and Muz Ibach on the porch of their winter home on Lemesurier Island across Icy Strait from Gustavus. Two smiling people with short gray-white hair stand next to each other. Joe is wearing hip waders and Muz wears what looks like a long dark skirt. Both are wearing men's shirts, the top buttons tight at the neck. Joe is taller than Muz.

In the photograph, Muz is holding onto Joe's arm. She looks straight into the camera lens, leaning in toward him. Joe appears to be making a joke, his head slightly cocked to one side.

At night in my bunk, I studied that picture, taken in 1954 by former park staff ranger Bruce Black. I see humor, joy, and light in Muz's eyes and Joe's, like sunlight reflected on saltwater.

QUESTIONS

Why did I want to know the Ibachs, although they were no longer alive? Was I looking for parents who loved each other, for courage, a model for standing on my own? Was I seeking a way to find inner strength and to live a practical life? I looked back then for a way out of violent relationships and years of depression punctuated by a few moments of LSD- and mescaline-fueled beauty. I sought experiences where I could see the presence of every cell and the light inside of everything.

In my twenties, I took peyote on a Colorado mountain. I remember the smell of earth. I took LSD in a St. Louis Victorian house where we listened to music played on old LP records, and the music made visible to me a whole span of the history of the world. I took mescaline on the banks of the Missouri River, where a friend and I danced on a hillside surrounded by the falling leaves of wild persimmon, oak and sumac. In those years when everything seemed dark, with my mother in mental wards, I needed to know that wonder still existed, that beauty was not gone from the world.

I'd been in two violent relationships in my late twenties, including a couple of nights I was lucky to survive. I provoked one man by disappearing from a house we shared without telling him where I was going. He had already threatened me. I said I'd be back in a few minutes. I returned late that night after spending all day in the mountains with another man.

"If you want to die, why don't you do it yourself?" said a friend of his and mine. She made a reservation, drove me to the airport, and put me on a plane.

"You have to get out of here," she said.

Left to my own devices, I would have stayed while the whole scenario played out.

Of course, that plane ride didn't stop me. I found another relationship, worse than the first, with a man who took drugs. He stabbed his own leg with a knife so I wouldn't make him leave. I couldn't yet be trusted to take care of my own life.

6   One night when the two of us were fighting, a wise neighbor knocked on the door.

"If you want to argue, come to my house," she announced as she led me away. He came to the neighbor's house with his friend.

"Leave her alone. She has enough to deal with," his friend said. They left the neighbor's house, and I stayed. I had just found out that I was pregnant, although he had told me that he'd had a vasectomy.

I chose not to have the child. I thought that, if I gave birth, I would never be able to escape him. I didn't want him to follow me. I didn't want that for my child. He could have found me but didn't. I measure my strength from that time. I had moved from a domineering father in a wheelchair to violent men who could walk. After a few years of boring jobs in Seattle, I went to be a housekeeper in Glacier Bay, where the dangers came, not from other people, but from waves and ice and bears.

So a couple who lived alone together in Reid Inlet and Lemesurier Island, who were renowned for their hospitality and love, the epitome of a perfect couple, were people I envied and admired. I looked to the thread of their lives as a way to nourish my soul and to ground it in reality. I left the places and people I knew for a life in Alaska that looked crazy to my family, both as a way to get even with my parents and a way to heal myself.

SUMMER 1974

I arrived at the Gustavus airport from Seattle my first year in Glacier Bay on the afternoon jet. The plane flew north over Puget Sound above waters that stretch for a thousand miles through fjords and islands carved by ice during a series of ice ages. As it often does, the weather changed as we flew over the *Haida Gwaii*, (Islands of the People), at that time called the Queen Charlottes. There was sun in Seattle, but clouds filled the skies in Alaska as we passed above Ketchikan and Wrangell. In the south, the forests were Douglas fir and red cedar; in the north, hemlock, yellow cedar and Sitka spruce.

That spring, on Bainbridge Island across Puget Sound half an hour by ferry from Seattle, I read a sign posted on a bulletin board: "Work in Alaska. $3.00 an hour." It was reasonable pay for Seattle at the time but low by Alaska standards.

At my interview, I asked the Glacier Bay Lodge manager, "Is there a way to earn more money?"

"You can be the head housekeeper," she said, "and we'll pay you another thirty-five cents an hour." She didn't ask if I had supervised people. I didn't tell her I hadn't.

I grew up in the 1950s in a middle class Jewish family in St. Louis. I knew how to iron and sweep, but a series of African-American women, hired as maids by my mother to do housekeeping, childcare and cooking, made my bed. In Bartlett Cove that first summer, I learned the details of folding the corners of sheets and mopping floors in bathrooms from the wife of a Bartlett Cove maintenance man and a fourth generation Gustavus homesteader who was part of the crew I supervised. That summer I evened out my karma, making beds to compensate for all the beds that others had made for me. I learned the best way to conserve the toilet paper supply, by putting the roll on the spool so that it unrolled from the back.

In those years, Lodge guests and employees ate watery green beans and peas and carrots from cans, long before the days when fresh vegetables came north on the planes that took fresh salmon south. The town of Gustavus had no store. Supplies for the Lodge came by boat in the spring from Seattle. At mid-summer, there might be a

COLD MOUNTAIN MORNING: GUSTAVUS BEACH AND THE FAIRWEATHER RANGE, 2011

Copyright Fritz Koschmann.

barge. Those supplies had to last until the end of the season. The alternative was to order replacements from Juneau and pay the expense of freight. At the Lodge, they skimped on supplies if they could and jerry-rigged anything that broke. The only fresh vegetables at the Lodge in those years were a few shreds of iceberg lettuce on a plate with a gob of Thousand Island dressing. By my second week, I was fed up with eating canned spaghetti and frozen French fries.

One evening I stopped the manager on the front steps of the Lodge and unloaded my complaint that the food was no good and that it was making me ill.

She said, "If you have special requirements, you shouldn't have come to Alaska. Stop complaining or leave." She was matter of fact, not angry, so it wasn't quite an ultimatum. But where would I go? Not back to my dead-end job in Seattle. I wasn't interested in another job search. At first I was upset, but I thought about it and decided to stop complaining.

I ate meals in the staff dining room until I was too sick to work, in mid-July. Then I went to Juneau by small plane. The diagnosis was easy for the doctor.

He said, "Too little roughage in your diet," a usual Alaska ailment in those days. Fresh vegetables were hard to come by, except for those grown by homesteaders. Their gardens grew well, nourished by the rain and long summer days and the kelp they gathered on the beach, but the homesteaders in Gustavus in those years grew only enough for themselves.

I bought oil, flour, honey and eggs and a few vegetables at the grocery store in Juneau. Back in Bartlett Cove, I cooked meals in an employee trailer. At low tide, I walked across the mudflats near Lagoon Island to dig cockles. I wore tall red rubber boots, known as "Juneau tennies" because, like tennis shoes in warmer climates at that time, people wore them everywhere. We rolled the tops down for hiking on rock, moss, and gravel and rolled them back up to wade. Wearing those boots meant I fit in.

SUMMER 1974

That summer I gathered beach greens, strawberries and blueberries. I picked shaggy mane mushrooms near the path to the dock. I baked fresh bread in the trailer and traded with fishermen who anchored out in Bartlett Cove for fresh salmon and halibut.

I walked the beaches and learned to tell what an animal had eaten by looking at the color of its scat. Dark blue in the bear scat meant blueberries; light grey hair in coyote scat meant mice. Like them, I was simply one more mammal browsing my way through the landscape.

I saw hummingbirds near the Lodge and eagles overhead. I paid attention to time and tide. I watched seals, puffins, grebes, cormorants and phalaropes as well as orca and humpback whales. Once, cleaning a Lodge cabin, I found a sleeping bat hanging by its toes from a curtain rod. I pried its feet loose, took it in my hands, and deposited it on the railing outside.

Some days, after work, I walked the Bartlett Cove beach or listened to tourists' stories by the fireplace in the lobby. After dinner, I watched park naturalists' slide programs. Other evenings I sat with fishermen and rangers as they discussed where the salmon were running, whose motor broke down, and how long it would take to get parts. Commercial fishing was still allowed in Glacier Bay then, so lots of fishermen anchored up in Bartlett Cove and spent the night in the Lodge's bar.

When the weather was good, I sat outside on the deck and gazed at Mt. Fairweather, Mt. Crillon, and Mt. Bertha, while the sun set among the snow-covered peaks. By the end of the summer, I could play a few chords on my guitar, but every night I wrote in the journal.

Who was this long ago woman, this "I"? I came to Glacier Bay at age thirty, alone and adrift.

"A crab is easy to take out of the shell," I wrote in the journal. "Hold the claws, catch the edge over something, and push down. The shell comes off, and you can break the crab in half. The blind woman was so still yesterday trying to find her room that I thought something was wrong. She was just listening with her eyes closed. That is what I do, too, when I want to know."

Like all of us, I was a composite. We are cells that divide, hold a shape and dissolve. We are made of water and cells and stories.

BROWN BEARS, REID INLET, 2007

Copyright Fritz Koschmann.

ICE COUNTRY

Everything changes in Glacier Bay. The height of the mountains isn't fixed. One tectonic plate, the Pacific, pushes under the North American plate at the edge of the continent, and the tension creates periodic earthquakes that lift up the mountain peaks. This shift along the Fairweather Fault on Glacier Bay's outer coast, a continuation of the San Andreas, is similar to the process that pushed up the Himalayas. Under different names, the San Andreas Fault circles from Tierra del Fuego to Anchorage and beyond. It crosses the Bering Sea to Kamchatka and curls south past Japan to New Zealand.

The main benefit of working at Glacier Bay Lodge was weekly free tour boat trips up the Bay on days off. In addition, I wandered the Bartlett Cove dock and wheedled invitations for trips up the bay on private powerboats and sailboats. It was easy, in the mid-1970s, to get off a boat in the upper part of Muir Inlet, near Forest Creek, Goose Cove or Wolf Point, and to walk for miles over bare gravel and rock with no trees to stop you. It's not that you didn't need a map, but a person could set a goal and simply hike toward it cross-country, before the alders grew up along the ground so thick that it took hours to get through them. I touched the stumps of trees cut down by glaciers during the Little Ice Age and washed out by melt water streams when the ice disappeared. According to radiocarbon dating, the ancient forest was buried under gravel three thousand years before I stood there.

The physical history of this place results not only from being shaped by ice but from slow accumulation as well—layers of sediment forming into rock, deposits of glacial till, gravel shaping the sea beds, pollen preserved in ice where it fell. After being depressed by the weight of ice, the land of Glacier Bay is rising up, rebounding, in the aftermath of glacial retreat.

A camera doesn't capture all of the land's motion. Land shifts on the surface and beneath. The deep change occurs below what we can see, in slow geologic motion. The rock layers also move horizontally, in lateral shifts. Rocks in the upper west arm of Glacier Bay were once found at the latitude where Mexico now lies. This bay was not always a bay, and these rocks were not always here.

A myriad of species live in Glacier Bay. The place is transformed by what passes through it, by ice, by rivers, by rain and by otters in the rivers and seas, by porcupines in the undergrowth, by wolverines. What is left in a place becomes part of it—gravel, wind-blown leaves, the droppings of mice, the scat of humans and weasels and bears; seeds carried by wind, fur and human clothing; a grain of sand, a feather. Plants rise from the land and die into it, creating layers of soil: dwarf fireweed, lupine, alder, cottonwood, spruce and hemlock, marsh marigold and Kamchatka lilies. The contents of our bodies change shape, too, as their elements aggregate and dissolve.

I saw thousands of the birds that migrate through Glacier Bay, nesting in its forests, rock islands, and shores or moving through it on their way north: pigeon guillemots, oystercatchers with their red bills and pink feet; Canada geese, red-throated loons, marbled murrelets, killdeer, kingfishers, ravens and crows, goldeneye and ptarmigan. I could identify the sea birds by their color, location, by their shape and patterns of flight: the short fat black puffin with white markings and curved beak, the cormorant drying outstretched wings, the merganser sleek and low on the water. There were rafts of phalaropes in the lower bay. Arctic terns, which fly twenty-two thousand miles in their annual migration, circled near icebergs at a glacier's face each spring and flew back to the Antarctic in the fall. I watched them flying and gliding with angled wings and could differentiate terns from small gulls called kittiwakes. I saw eagles catch salmon in the Beardslee Islands. I knew the call of the hermit thrush. When migrating sandhill cranes circled above Gustavus, everyone in town ran outside to look up and stopped what they were doing to listen.

I saw humpback whales, seals, porpoises, and sea otters swimming. At low tide, I gazed at starfish and crabs, sea urchins, clams, cockles and mussels. I watched brown bears and black bears, although no brown bears up close. I saw coyotes eating halibut entrails and heard wolves in the night in Gustavus. For all of these species, Glacier Bay is their biosphere and habitat.

I saw harbor seals that birthed their pups on icebergs to protect them from roving orca. I knew that, in the presence of boats in the ice, the mothers and newborn pups would slide off the icebergs and scatter. Afterwards, some harbor seal mothers and pups might not be able to locate each other.

In 1974, twelve glaciers flowed down to the sea in Glacier Bay proper. The first few summers I was there, Muir Glacier retreated so rapidly that a boat had to navigate through six miles of floating ice to reach it, if the skipper dared. Icebergs, some the size of houses, floated fifty miles south into Icy Strait. By 2014, only six of the inner bay's glaciers still reached tidewater.

After a few summers, I could recognize most of the bay's glaciers in photos based upon the slope, width and silhouette of the ice face, the shapes of the surrounding mountains, and the trajectory of the ice flow. My preferred mode of spending time anywhere in Glacier Bay was to sit, close my eyes and then open them as a way to get my bearings. I spent most of my time up there gazing. Once at Point Gustavus, just sitting, I saw ravens fly upside down in a westerly wind.

The mystics of all religions see everything in the world as one and indivisible, as did the philosopher Spinoza. The Jewish mystics say that there is a hidden spark within everything we see. These sparks come from the lost *Shekhinah*, the feminine aspect of God. The male aspect, they say, is distant and withdrawn. Our job is to reunite them, to liberate the sparks. Being close to the *Shekhinah* is to be in a place where God's whole presence is felt.

I wanted to be at the heart of that place; I wanted to become it, as if I could be at one with every bird and bivalve. I would attempt, without quite noticing, to feel their motion in my muscles and bones, how it felt to be a barnacle closing with the tide, how it felt to swoop and dive like a bird, as if I were the spirit of the place that held all those millions of expressions of life. I could feel that Glacier Bay's intrinsic energy differed from the stable energy I sensed sitting on a brick levee by the Mississippi River, although the state of Missouri also lies in an earthquake zone.

There's no way to be all of the experience of Glacier Bay in one woman's body, and making the attempt seems far from humble. The people who know Glacier Bay well all value humility, in a place where it's clear that a human being is one tiny speck in that huge landscape.

Still, my body and my heart within my skin seemed to be trying to match the vastness around me, as if this expansion was the way to discover the essence of that place and what it might have to tell me.

Ice Country is moving, shifting and changing.

Ice country is alive.

MIGRATION

I don't know the exact location in Eastern Europe from which my portion of the Jewish tribe migrated west in ships. Their original home was Galicia, probably the town of Nowy Sacz, now in Poland. The last way station for my father's family was Antwerp, the city of his birth. He came from a family of Jewish peasants, a few specks in the outward migration escaping poverty and prejudice and avoiding service in the army of the emperor of Austria-Hungary. They rode steerage three thousand miles across the Atlantic to Nova Scotia. They passed through immigration from Canada to the United States with five children and their feather beds in an early twentieth-century wave of immigrants from a world of Jewish villages and ghettos that no longer exists.

My father's family arrived in St. Louis in the year 1914, thousands of years after Tlingit people first arrived in Glacier Bay, thirty-five years after John Muir searched for a glacial landscape to compare with Yosemite Valley and first saw the great glacier that was later named after him. My father's family came to a land of two rivers, the Missouri and the Mississippi, just before the outbreak of World War I. When my father arrived in the U.S., he was three years old.

My mother's parents came from Ukraine, the province of Kiev. She was born in St. Louis in 1919. When my brothers and I were children, she loved to take us "out to the country" in the rolling Missouri hills, to a summer camp where we slept in hammocks, or to the Ralston Purina test farm. By age ten, I could identify Virginia creeper, sassafras, persimmon, dogwood, rosebud and poison ivy. I could row a boat and paddle a canoe. On Sunday drives in the Missouri countryside, I looked out car windows and traced the shapes of the rounded old mountains and valleys, the limestone bluffs of the Mississippi, the clear Ozark rivers spilling over rocks and bordered by wild roses and willows. For as long as I can remember, land and its shape were important to me. I never quite bonded with my mother, who seemed emotionally far away, but I think I bonded with the shape of the earth and the soft curves of those hills.

We lived at the southernmost boundary of the great Pleistocene glaciers, although I did not know that fact. I remember reading about fjords, the narrow steep-sided sea inlets created by glaciers, in our second grade newspaper, *The Weekly Reader*. The single second grade fact I remember was that fjords were found in Norway. I didn't know that glaciers also carved fjords in Greenland and Iceland and Sweden, in Patagonia (Chile and Argentina), and in New Zealand, Canada and Alaska.

I stopped taking piano lessons at age eleven to go back to Hebrew School. I wanted to have a bat mitzvah ceremony. I thought it was the way to become a woman. I wanted to deliver a speech I wrote in front of the congregation, but our traditional rabbi required that each child, boy or girl, memorize a speech the rabbi had written. In my own case, the speech he wrote was about Deborah, a judge in Israel who led armies.

"Follow me," she said to the general Barak, "and we will be victorious."

At age twelve, I was a writer. I woke up in the night with poems. I stopped writing poetry at age thirteen, after my bat mitzvah, thinking I had no permission to speak.

In college, I wrote literature research papers. I'd visit a professor in his office. He would hand me the paper with a grade on the cover, usually an A or A-. More than one professor added a note that said something like: "Why did you write this paper?"

I would look down, stare at the question and shrug, thank the professor and leave. In those years, my school had no female professors. I wrote papers because these men assigned them. What other reason could there be?

When I was a freshman in college, my mother was diagnosed as bipolar. She was in and out of hospitals. Two years later, I had what was called a nervous breakdown, and I left school and went home to St. Louis. I could sit at my desk and type one word, then another, but I could no longer shape a train of thought into a whole literature paper because I couldn't make the words I typed form themselves into sentences.

LEARNING TO KAYAK

July 1974. Bartlett Cove. I am paddling in calm water with a man who is teaching me to kayak. We float with the tide through the cut that leads into the emerald-colored inner lagoon. He is steering from the back of the kayak, and I am in the front. It is early evening and cloudy, but it isn't raining. In Glacier Bay, that is considered good weather.

"Straighten your forearm and push the paddle forward rather than pulling your arm back," he instructs. The boat is a Klepper, an inflatable sea kayak that is stable in waves, although, this night, there are none. I begin to get the hang of it. The ripples from the movements of our paddles, bolstered by the current and a light wind, carry us. Kayaking is a new tourist activity this year. I met this guide because I tried to meet everyone who looked interesting that summer I worked at the Lodge. I was the head housekeeper, which gave me a kind of status.

"What do you do besides clean cabins?" I hear his question from the back of the kayak, and I know it isn't a put-down. He isn't denigrating my position; this is a place where the willingness and capacity to do physical work are valued above riches or academic knowledge.

I hadn't shown anyone my writing that summer or said I was keeping a journal. I hadn't shared my own poetry since, as a girl of ten or eleven, I wrote poetry hiding under the covers so that my parents wouldn't know I was awake. Writing had always been a secret activity for me.

I gave up writing at puberty, when poems in the night stopped appearing. I fell into a life like that of the girl who pricked her finger with a spindle and fell asleep in fairy tales, waiting for the prince. When I tried to write poetry in college, I couldn't find words that came from inside, as if my soul had dried up and there was no one within me to find.

I could have told the man kayaking with me that I hiked and watched birds and was learning to play the guitar. Those answers were true on the surface. But the real answer was that I was keeping in a journal, my first writing in many years. Sleeping Beauty was awakening, even if it wasn't yet clear that the only person who could wake me up was myself.

"I am keeping a journal," I heard myself tell him. I couldn't lie in that pure salt air.

He asked a second question, carefully. It was: "Would you let me read it?"

Had I recorded my summer attractions to a ranger and to a fellow Lodge employee? Did I write of the times when those desires had been and had not been fulfilled? Oh, well. In the mid 1970s, in the wake of the hippie years and before the AIDS epidemic, my sexual behavior with men that summer would not have been very shocking. I might as well be courageous. I gave him the journal that evening.

A few days later, on the porch of the Lodge, he returned the journal to me.

"This writing is good," he said, and I found that I believed him. I hadn't been looking for feedback, but his comment seemed to nourish a seed long buried, frozen within me.

It was nearly the end of the summer and almost time to go south.

"What will I do this winter?" I wondered. I had no job.

"I can be a writer," I thought, and the thought rang true.

Two months later, in October, living on Bainbridge Island, I got a temp job in a Seattle office and rode the ferry daily to the city. Bored with typing other people's reports and letters, as secretaries did in those days, and tired of taking directions, I sent a list of feature article ideas to the editor of *The Bainbridge Review*, the island's weekly newspaper. I wrote first an article about a sailboat race in which I participated. Our island sailing club, which raced all winter as long as the wind wasn't too strong, won a Saturday morning race against the big Seattle yachts.

For the next two years, I wrote feature articles. I came up with the topics myself: a women's clinic, beekeeping, composting toilets, a local farm that raised quail and pheasants for high end Seattle restaurants. After that, I thought it was time to graduate to a different format.

"I can go back to Glacier Bay," I thought. "I will write for magazines."

BECOMING A WRITER

On my first day of Sunday school, at age five, I walked up the hill from our house in St. Louis to YMHA (Young Men's Hebrew Association) near the corner of Delmar and Union Street. My class met there while our new synagogue was under construction. The class was three floors up, at the top of long flights of stairs.

We drew pictures with crayons. I drew grass and trees on a wide piece of paper and God in the right hand corner. My mother read fairy tales to me at bedtime from a book with gilded illustrations of men with long beards who represented the winds of the north, south, east and west. I must have thought that I knew how God looked. I showed my finished drawing to the teacher. I was so proud of myself!

"But if you're Jewish, you can't draw a picture of God," said the teacher from behind her wooden desk. It was an old tradition, protection from idol worship coming down through the centuries.

I walked home holding my rolled up drawing. I didn't show it or tell my parents. What was the point of having paper and crayons, if I couldn't draw God? I reached the kind of silent conclusion that a Talmudic scholar might discover: *If I can't draw God, I will write.*

I told everyone I was a writer my second summer in Glacier Bay, but I couldn't put words on a page.

"How's it going?" was the daily question from the park rangers and lodge employees. "Have you written anything yet?" Glacier Bay's humpback whale researcher, Chuck Jurasz, suggested writing a book together about how visitors saw Glacier Bay. His idea was to interview kayakers, sailors, cruise ship passengers. I declined his offer, afraid of the power of his intellect. Carol Janda said that "Sometimes the light comes in horizontal," and we talked about why I was stuck, but Carol, married to Chief Ranger Chuck Janda, was a potter and a painter. She wasn't a writer.

By August, I was desperate.

REID GLACIER DWARFING VISITORS, 2006
Copyright Fritz Koschmann.

Dave Bohn, the photographer and author of *The Land and the Silence*, arrived in Bartlett Cove a few days before what came to be called the "bear incident." A brown bear killed a hiker on White Thunder Ridge, a place where you could still hear the sound of three tidewater glaciers calving: the Muir, McBride and Riggs.

I left a note on the door of the trailer in Bartlett Cove where Dave Bohn was living. The park staff had asked him to help monitor the radio during the search for the lost camper because the small staff was needed for the search, and at that time Dave Bohn knew Glacier Bay almost as well as anyone.

Bohn met me in one of the two new park staff residences. We spent half an hour together. Why was I unable to write? Dave had two explanations.

First: "If that wall were a bookshelf filled with books about Alaska, how many would contain new ideas? Most would be full of second- and third-hand information. You want to say something new. That takes time. The way to get to know a place is to spend time with it."

Second: "The articles you were planning to write would be like selling the place. You want to give something back." As if I wanted to truly see the place and to be generous, as if he trusted me before I knew that I could trust myself.

We had a follow-up conversation a few days later, in the small building near the inner lagoon that housed the park superintendent's office.

With the buzz of the shortwave radio in the background, the two of us came up with three questions: "Why do people come here? Why do they stay or return?" And: "What can be learned from a place like this?" (Of course, those questions didn't cover the experience of Tlingit people, who have made this place home for hundreds of years.)

Dave said, "When a well-known person in academia retires, colleagues write essays to celebrate that person's contributions." In German, that sort of book is called a *festschrift*. It means "a celebration in writing." In Latin it is called an *encomium*, "a glowing and warmly enthusiastic praise—a eulogy, a tribute, a panegyric, an accolade, a commendation, an homage, a paean, a hymn."

I didn't know it then, but Dave Bohn must have known that those three questions included me: why did I come and return and what could I learn. Was that Dave's joke?

I have spent time periodically in Glacier Bay over more than forty years, although never forty nights in a tent like Dave. I spent time in Glacier Bay in short bursts and the rest in Seattle and Portland. In Glacier Bay I could find an inner space quiet enough that I could actually see what was outside: the Kamchatka lily, the sea urchin, the coyote, the riptides, the land's shape, the heron.

THE IBACHS' CABIN

I first saw the Ibachs' cabin in Reid Inlet close up in the summer of 1976. It was the U.S. bicentennial year. I had shipped two of everything north to Gustavus: a down sleeping bag for warmth and a polyester sleeping bag for rain; a backpacking tent and a wall tent; light and heavy rain gear; two wool hats, two sets of gloves. It took me five days to build the courage to camp overnight alone in Reid Inlet. I was well equipped but not brave.

I finally stepped onto the deck of the tour boat on a cloudy June day with no rain. I rode into Glacier Bay's West Arm with one hundred or more park visitors and a Park Service naturalist. She pointed out differences in the predominant species of vegetation as we moved up the bay: spruce and hemlock forests near Bartlett Cove; cottonwoods farther north; then alders and willows. Going north we moved as if slipping backwards in time: seeing land as it looked two hundred years after the ice melted; how it looked after one hundred years; after fifty; and then after ten. On our right as we turned into Reid Inlet was the Ibachs' cabin near the spit; three miles ahead was Reid Glacier with bare rock and gravel at its face. We moved through grey-green water filled with glacial till and icebergs, all remnants of the Little Ice Age.

The boat stopped not far from the glacier's face, and a crewmember rowed me ashore. Reid Glacier, advancing, slid forward that year on a seabed of gravel and mud. I stood on the beach alone and watched the dinghy pull away. I hauled my gear up to a rock about half a mile from the glacier. Then I walked down the gravel beach.

The cabin, built of grey weathered boards, was leaning by then at an angle. It was stable, propped up by a four-by-four on one side. I was hesitant to enter. I could sense the Ibachs' presence, although I knew they were no longer alive. I only knew about them from Dave Bohn's book. I knew that Joe Ibach's family was German, that he and Muz raised foxes on Middleton Island in Prince William Sound before they moved to Lemesurier Island near the mouth of Glacier Bay, and that the actor John Barrymore had visited them on his yacht.

I stepped slowly into the cabin's mudroom, a closed-in entry space built for taking off muddy boots and hanging up dripping rain gear. Swallows had built a nest on a hanging

REID GLACIER AND THE
IBACH CABIN GROUP
SERIES, 1985
Copyright Robert E. Howe.
Courtesy of Fred Howe.

saw just inside, and the floor was covered with feathers. One old boot lay in the corner. It felt strange to walk in uninvited, despite the fact that I'd heard that all who came to visit them were welcome.

The Ibachs had built the mudroom from boards nailed upright in vertical strips. I noticed paint on one board to my left just inside the door. I tilted my head to the right. That paint formed the top halves of written letters. I couldn't read what they said. On a second board, nailed next to the first, I saw the bottom halves of the letters. I tilted my head to the left. The bottom halves faced away, in the opposite direction. I finally puzzled it out.

The nearest stores were in Juneau and Seattle. That meant shipment by plane, boat or barge. In Alaska, people took apart old buildings. Some left old cars and trucks in their yards, to cannibalize them for spare parts. In Alaska, little is wasted.

The mudroom of the Ibachs' cabin was built from old scavenged boards. Most likely they came from an abandoned fish cannery in Idaho Inlet or Cross Sound. Those boards were the cannery's "no trespassing" sign, in an earlier incarnation. Their message was meant to keep people out. The Ibachs no doubt took the old boards to their winter home on Lemesurier by boat and then, on their trip north in spring, to Reid Inlet fifty miles by barge. They nailed the boards into the cabin so the letters faced inside, their unwelcoming message illegible. The word "passing" was all I could read.

Was that Ibach practicality? Ibach humor? Ibach philosophy?

I stepped into the cabin's narrow main room. A small table was nailed to the wall—no space for legs in a kitchen so tiny. Above the table, photographs covered the wall: a page from Arizona Highways, with a color photo of sandstone and cactus; clippings of a chicken coop and chickens; pictures of clothing (jodhpurs and jackets) from a Montgomery Ward catalog. On a single wallpaper square, a drawing of a southern plantation home with grass lawns, dormers and porches.

I stepped into a second room, smaller than the first. At the far end was a window built for its view of the glacier. Twin metal bed frames with metal springs stood on each side of the door. On the wall next to the bed on the right was a picture of a raven, head cocked, with a look like Joe's in its eye.

I walked outside and up the slope behind the cabin and sat down. The beauty of the day was around me. I breathed it in and breathed it out, closed my eyes and opened them.

I looked toward the door of the cabin. A thought floated through my mind. The word "EN-trance," a doorway, an opening, is the same word as "en-TRANCE," an opening into a different state of awareness. One meaning flowed into another with the simple shift in emphasis. Thoughts reconfigured. Meanings dissolved. Words didn't hold together. The light, the clear air and the sounds of the wind were the only mind-altering substances required, as effective as any hallucinogen.

In the evening I walked back up the beach toward the glacier and set up my tent on the knoll. I ate dinner at 11:00 p.m. and fell asleep about sunset. That night, I woke more than once. I heard the ice boom and creak, that signature sound of a glacier inching its way toward the sea. I heard cracks like cannon shots when ice from the glacier's face fell into the bay, as if the ice were a living thing.

I imagined Joe and Muz lying in those narrow beds on a rare clear night in late summer, with stars and no rain, in this land of literal transformation, where words shift and dissolve and are honed down to their essence.

I could see why the Ibachs would consider dying together after living together in that cabin.

I imagine they felt joy in being with each other all those years on Lemesurier Island and at Reid Inlet, that exquisite raw place, while the world lived through the Great Depression and World War II and its aftermath.

They must have laughed as the glacier calved and late summer moonlight covered them up like a blanket.

MOMENT IN TIME

At a Park Service meeting in June 1976 in the Bartlett Cove headquarters building, I asked, "Will the Park Service restore the Ibachs' cabin?" To me this seemed a brilliant idea. Glacier Bay was a national monument then. The number of staff in Bartlett Cove was tiny: five year-round staff—superintendent, chief ranger, Bartlett Cove ranger, chief naturalist, maintenance supervisor, and one maintenance staff person. The numbers swelled in summer by ten or fifteen: four seasonal rangers to patrol the whole bay plus the outer coast; a ranger for Bartlett Cove; more maintenance workers; and a few seasonal naturalists to give evening programs at the lodge, guide walks on Bartlett Cove trails, and point out birds, whales, and bears to passengers on cruise ships and the daily tour boat.

In the '70s, if you worked at the park or the Lodge or were around the village of Gustavus for long, you knew almost everybody, the way people do in any small town. The new park superintendent who replaced Bob Howe had already surprised me, a hesitant new writer, by telling me I could ask the staff members anything I chose because of "freedom of the press." (By 2013 about fifty permanent staff worked in Bartlett Cove, and the number increased in the summer by another hundred.)

"What would you do with the cabin?" the superintendent asked me at that meeting in 1976. What would I do if I were in his shoes? That's probably what he meant. Repair the cabin? Build a dock in Reid Inlet? Lead hikes down the beach to the glacier?

I didn't hear his question that way. I heard it more personally. What would *I* do with the Ibachs' cabin?

I knew I would live in Reid Inlet. It took me two days to admit this, to myself, but not to him. Living in Reid Inlet would never be permitted according to park regulation.

Most park staff at the meeting did not believe in restoring the cabin. They had discussed their philosophy of park management for years. They didn't believe in preservation. Leave that to historical parks, like George Washington's home at Mount Vernon or the Klondike Gold Rush Park in Skagway. Glacier Bay was set aside as a monument in 1925 in part on the basis of its value to science, as one of the few places in the world to study what occurred as glaciers melted: the order and timing in which plants and animals arrived, in the absence of human interference. Using studies in botany begun by William Skinner Cooper in 1916 and in geology by Dr. William O. Field in 1926, you could tell from what was growing in a place how long ago the ice had melted. Scientists began to contemplate the idea of human effects on climate in the early 19th century, but the scientific community in general did not acknowledge the deleterious effects of human actions on climate until the late 1980s.

At that 1976 Bartlett Cove meeting, one park staff member said, "Glacier Bay is not a museum."

"The Ibachs lived in Reid Inlet when the land was bare rock and gravel," said another. "It was easy to prospect then, when the veins in the rock were uncovered and visible. In a few years, willows and alder will cover everything. The reason for the cabin's existence will be gone."

The superintendent made a comment I remember. His words could be used to justify almost any use of the park, and I did not like that idea, but his statement also contained a literal truth.

He said, "We are not here to preserve any one moment in time." As if I would think that we could.

BEDROOM: INSIDE THE IBACHS' CABIN, REID INLET, MAY 1969

Copyright Dave Bohn.

REID GLACIER AND THE SEA, 2006
Copyright Fritz Koschmann.

MINING

In the summer of 1976, the issue of mining in national parks was once again before Congress. None of the gold mines in Glacier Bay were active, although a few people still held patented claims. The main threat came from a company with plans to tunnel for copper and nickel under the huge Brady Glacier and build a city of ten thousand people at Dixon Harbor on the outer coast. On one hand that idea seemed like a pipe dream, but people at the park were horrified. (The price of nickel and copper fell low enough that the mine wasn't viable, but the Brady Glacier claim still exists.)

Joe Ibach had been a prospector in Glacier Bay. His first year there was 1924. In summer, the Ibachs ferried what they needed up the bay to Reid Inlet by barge from their winter home on Lemesurier Island fifty miles away. They unloaded the boards for construction, the tools, and the bags of soil by hand at Reid Inlet, using wheelbarrow and shovel, to plant vegetables and strawberries. Each year in August or early September at the end of the short Reid Inlet summer, as the storms began and the days got shorter, the Ibachs filled the barge with gold ore by hand and took it south to Lemesurier to mill in winter.

Was the Park staff against protecting the Ibachs' cabin because staff members were opposed to mining? Ken Youmans was the Park's maintenance supervisor. He was sixty-six years old, wiry and strong, with white hair. In 1957, he had become the first Glacier Bay National Monument employee permanently stationed in Bartlett Cove. He knew Joe Ibach. Ken Youmans had been a prospector, too, on his days off, in his spare time.

"Did Joe Ibach want to make millions from the gold in Reid Inlet?" I asked him one cloudy Saturday afternoon when the Gustavus Inn was open to locals. Ken and I sat on adjoining bar stools. The inn was known for its homemade wine. I drank orange juice that day, but the Inn was a good place to socialize.

"Joe kept papers on his claims but never filed them," said Ken. "He advised me to do the same. That way people won't find out where your claim is and stake out a claim next to yours.

"He had everything he wanted," Ken said.

I found this hard to believe. I had never heard a statement like that from or about anyone in my life.

"But didn't he want to strike it rich and make money from his claims in Reid Inlet?" I asked.

"He had everything he wanted," Ken replied.

"Really?" I asked again, doubtful. Everyone I knew seemed ambitious, for money or fame or whatever seemed necessary.

Ken Youmans, known as a patient man, was almost impatient that day, but he said it one more time, slowly, for my benefit.

"He had *everything* he wanted."

SUICIDE PACT

Joe and Muz Ibach made a suicide pact. That story everyone knew. If one of them died, the Ibachs agreed, the other would commit suicide. Muz died of cancer in a Juneau hospital, and Joe shot himself on Lemesurier Island a year later, on a day when he was scheduled to return to Reid Inlet for the first time without her.

In Gustavus, it was easy to fall in love with people, with men, women and children. It was as if I could see their spirits. It was easier than in a city to see who people truly were in that small town, to meet them without distractions, to speak to them when they stopped to chat in the middle of the road. In the mid-1970s in Gustavus, people spoke of the Ibachs as if Muz and Joe had just stepped out of the room.

That story of suicide didn't stop me. I was still curious. I knew that Muz and Joe Ibach lived together, mostly alone, and that they loved each other. I was thirty years old when I heard of the Ibachs and the suicide pact, fifteen years after Muz died.

I knew there was something special about them, but I couldn't put my finger on it. I was an English major. I still thought a suicide pact was romantic. As if the Ibachs' story came from a novel. Before suicide attempts entered my life, ten years before my mother was suicidal and a man I married attempted to kill himself more than once. So much for romance!

MRS. WADE (LEFT) AND NELL CROWELL VISITING SOUTHEAST ALASKA, SUMMER 1937
Courtesy of Gustavus Historical Archives and Antiquities.

NELL PARKER

The land in Gustavus is rising, as it is in all of Glacier Bay. Geologists have a name for this phenomenon: isostatic rebound or, more recently, a less lyrical phrase, post-glacial adjustment. It's expected that land depressed by ice from the Pleistocene era will be rebounding for the next ten thousand years. The land of Glacier Bay is rebounding from the weight of several thousand feet of ice that covered it during the Little Ice Age. The outwash plain where Gustavus is built is also rising, like bread dough rebounds after you press a thumb into it.

I had already asked old-timer Archie Chase about the Ibachs one night while we sat with the heat cranked up in his mobile home near the river. Before Gustavus had electricity, you could hear his generator for miles. Archie, in his eighties, was related to many of the Gustavus homesteaders through his marriage to May Parker White.

"The Ibachs were strong people, special," he said. "But you'll find those characteristics in many older Alaskans."

"What's different about them?" I asked.

"That seems like a funny question to us," said Archie. It was a funny question, I agree—the question was too direct. Archie took his time, but he didn't shy away from it. He answered in his private vernacular with words left out of his sentences.

"We don't realize we're different," he said, "but I know we are; we know it. There's only one family Ruth and Fred Matson. There's only one family May and Archie. That's just the way it is. Long life up here, long winters, maybe just different from everybody else." I still didn't have my answer, but I think Archie was trying to say that people there took on their own true shapes.

So one summer afternoon I rode my bike to Nell and Glen Parker's house. Glen bulldozed that road into gravel left by the great glacier. Nell had invited me over for tea and to talk about Muz and Joe Ibach.

Nell was a small woman about sixty years old with graying hair and bright eyes. She wore a blouse with a flower pattern, gray pants and a wool sweater. The room had a large stone fireplace with a wooden mantel, and low-armed couches, oil lamps on wooden end tables, corner bookshelves and an old phonograph. The fireplace stone came from the beaches of Glacier Bay and the Parker mine at Ptarmigan Creek. I didn't know her well, but the natural thing to do was to sit on her couch while she showed me her photo albums. Nell had grown up in Clovis, California, south and east of San Jose.

Nell Crowell first came from California to Alaska at age twenty-three to assist a woman missionary. That seemed adventurous to me. Her plan was to teach vacation Bible school, but there were no children at the Excursion Inlet cannery that year. The missionary's boat broke down, and Leslie Parker and his brother Glen came around the point from Gustavus in their boat to make the repairs. They said, "You're so close. We will fix your boat if you will come to Gustavus to see our mother." They knew how to make a deal.

During that visit, the Parkers asked Nell to stay on in Gustavus as their mother's companion. Nell said she would go back to Juneau with the missionary, and she would return to Gustavus in ten days if someone could come to get her.

"When Glen picked me up in Juneau," Nell said, "he knocked on the door, and I thought he was forty years old. His beard nearly covered his face. He asked for 'that girl from California who is coming to stay with our mother.'" A photo from Nell's album showed her transportation when she returned to Gustavus to live: a group of smiling children on top of a pile of hay in back of an old truck driven out to the beach. I was sure Nell had told these stories before, but they were new to me.

The first night Nell was back in Gustavus, the Parkers had a party and made fudge. Glen Parker shaved off his beard that night, Nell said, "and he lost twenty years. I went out there in August," Nell told me, "and he gave me a ring in March."

Nell shows me another picture in the album. The missionary, a heavy-set woman, stands with Nell in front of a stand of spruce trees. The missionary wears a long white cotton dress. Nell is wearing a calf-length wool skirt with a pleat in front, a long-sleeved blouse that looks like silk, and a pin of cloth roses at the neck. I am surprised at how beautiful Nell looks. Of course, that photo was taken nearly forty years earlier.

The photograph is black-and-white, so I can't tell the color of Nell's clothes, but her shoes are white sandals with low heels. Perhaps the two women are going to church. Nell is smiling, her gaze is soft, and she looks elegant and composed. She wouldn't look out of place in the lobby of a San Francisco hotel.

Nell and Glen got married at the old Parker place on the banks of the Good River, she told me, showing me photos of the wedding. Her mother sent satin and lace, and Nell sewed her own wedding dress and silk slip.

"I thought you had to have satin for a wedding," Nell told me. She sewed lace on the edge of the slip.

I look at Nell and Glen in the photo, looking happy and young, in the doorway of the old Parker homestead. Nell's dress is draped and gathered at the bodice, and it falls straight to the hem. That dress she made looks like the work of a professional seamstress. Nell had a sense of fashion. A garland of lupine hangs around the doorframe of the house, with a wedding bell suspended from the middle.

I knew right off, because lupine was blooming, that the wedding must have been in June. Nell told me that the minister brought flowers for her bouquet when he came out on the wedding day from Juneau. They held the wedding feast outdoors with guests seated at a long table. It was cloudy, but it wasn't raining. The caption on the photo notes that the bride and groom served cake and hand-cranked ice cream. I once heard that Nell said, "I didn't marry a man. I married Alaska." The date of the wedding was June 10, 1938. I don't usually like looking at photos if I don't know people well, but Nell's album was history.

Glen grew up in Gustavus. He built that house for Nell on his homestead. He and his brothers dug miles of ditches to drain standing water over the years. That water covered much of Gustavus, before the Parker brothers drained it and before the land rose. The land in Gustavus is rising now at about the same rate that the level of the sea is increasing as a result of climate change and worldwide glacial melting.

On one end of Nell's living room was a large pump organ played by Nell's mother-in-law at Nell and Glen's wedding. Nell told me that, through a bank of windows looking out on a garden with wild roses, you could see at one time the waters of Icy Strait, "before all the trees grew up. Glen used to cut the trees back, but then it all got away from him." That meant you could see across to Lemesurier, before the spruce trees grew one hundred feet tall. The road to the Parkers' house is now officially called Glen's Ditch Road. I looked out the window and saw so many tall trees that it was hard to imagine bare land sixty years earlier.

Glen had a third-grade education, if that, but I knew he could fix anything. I saw him around town, a stocky figure wearing denim overalls, a flannel shirt, and tall rubber boots or a pair of slip-on fisherman's shoes. He spent much of his time fiddling with tools in his shed or bent over a truck engine or a boat motor. In one well-known Gustavus story, Glen got tired of flat tires on his tractor, so he filled the tires with concrete. How would he pour concrete into a tire? Maybe he mixed it thin. The hole in the tire would have to be big, but no problem, since the concrete would harden and seal it. He wouldn't have to worry about leaks, because a tire couldn't leak if it wasn't filled with air. Glen was famous for his love of machines.

For their honeymoon, Nell and Glen went up Glacier Bay in a boat that Glen and Les Parker built called the L & G. On their way up bay, the newlyweds dropped off supplies at the Leroy mine at Ptarmigan Creek, where Les was prospecting. Ptarmigan Creek is just west of Reid Inlet, around the point. Later, Glen built his own boat. He combined his name with Nell's and named the boat the Glenellen. I didn't think to ask Nell if she liked having a boat named after her.

"That summer, in July, just after our wedding," Nell told me, "my brother-in-law Les found a rich vein of gold. Once they handed me a flake of gold, and I dropped it in a crack in the floor. They tore up that floor to find it! I went to the Leroy mine every summer, I think, until 1950," Nell said. "That was when the vein wore out and Les sold the mine. We used to meet Joe and Muz in Icy Strait and tie our boats together to go up the Bay. Once it was snowing so hard up there in Glacier Bay that the snow didn't melt when it hit the water, and you could hear the boat, swish, swish, going through. We were afraid of hitting an iceberg.

"One time, before I trusted Glen so much in a boat, we went to see Muz and Joe in Reid Inlet," Nell told me. "We had to go through the narrow entrance to the inlet and then into the Ibachs' pothole." (In Southeast Alaska they use the word pothole in two ways: on land it's a hole in the road that tears up car and bike tires; in saltwater, it's a small pond or pool where you can anchor a boat. A pothole is too big to be called a puddle, and not big enough to be called a cove.) At high tide you could take your boat straight into the Ibachs' pothole, and there would still be water in it when the tide went out.

Nell said, "That was the first time I went there. I was afraid of getting close to the glacier. But Glen said, 'ah, it's two miles away.' Muz had told us they would hang a lantern so we could see where the pothole was. We rounded the corner to Reid Inlet and anchored. I was never so glad to see a light."

Nell told me this story long after it happened, but I felt her sense of relief.

GATHERING HAY ON THE GUSTAVUS BEACH IN LES PARKER'S TRUCK NEAR THE SITE OF THE PRESENT-DAY DOCK, 1937

Taking photo (shadow), Les Parker. In truck bed: Nell Crowell (wearing hat, standing in back); Henrietta White (dressed in black with white hat, sitting); Dorothy White (wearing black with black hat); Gloria White (wearing white blouse, standing); Genevieve White (wearing white blouse, sitting); Ed White (in black, standing); Alice White (wearing hood, or arm over face); Anne White (child with short, dark hair sitting next to Alice White). Courtesy of Gustavus Historical Archives and Antiquities.

GLEN PARKER ALONGSIDE HIS FIRST DITCH, LOOKING NORTH FROM THE GUSTAVUS BEACH TOWARDS THE BEARTRACK MOUNTAINS, 1930S
Courtesy of Gustavus Historical Archives and Antiquities.

WEDDING DAY OF NELL CROWELL AND GLEN PARKER AT THE HOME OF EDITH A. AND ABRAHAM LINCOLN PARKER, GUSTAVUS, JUNE 10, 1938

Back row L to R: Leslie Parker, Charles Parker, Jennie Parker, Bert Parker. Front row L to R: Edith A. Parker, Glen Parker, Nell (Crowell) Parker, Abraham Lincoln Parker, May (Parker) White. Courtesy of Gustavus Historical Archives and Antiquities.

JOE AND MUZ IBACH WITH GLEN PARKER, LEMESURIER ISLAND, 1940S

Photograph by Nell Parker, Courtesy of Gustavus Historical Archives and Antiquities.

JOE IBACH, REID INLET, AUGUEST 18, 1936

Photograph by John C. Reed, Sr., U.S. Geological Survey. Courtesy of USGS.

MOUND OF PANSIES

"Glen and I used to go to Lemesurier Island for a week at a time to help the Ibachs," Nell told me as we sat at her kitchen table. No doubt Nell, who was known as a seamstress, had made the red kitchen curtains. Mail order was available in the early days of Gustavus, but who would order anything that they could make themselves? Why give up the joy of ordering the fabric and waiting for it to arrive; of measuring and cutting and stitching with your own hands in winter while the rain or snow fell outside? There was also the need to be frugal. Nell probably didn't sew in summer, when there would be too many other things to do.

"Muz was in her mid-50s when I first met them, and Joe was about 60," Nell said to me that afternoon in her kitchen. "When you're twenty-three, that seems pretty old." The kitchen had homemade cabinets painted off-white, plus a sink, a small table, and a hand pump for water. The old wood cook stove had a teakettle simmering and old irons sitting on it. The water table in Gustavus was so high that all you had to do to get water was drive a pipe into the ground.

"The Ibachs grew flowers at Lemesurier Island for the pleasure of it," Nell told me, "and for the pleasure it gave other people. Their knives and forks had ivory handles made in England. They had good things, but, unless you knew how to recognize good things, you wouldn't know it." Joe Ibach was born on December 27, 1879 in Erie County, New York. Muz was born in Guelph, Ontario, Canada on March 5, 1885. They married in Cordova, Alaska, in 1908.

"Muz wore a certain kind of pants," Nell said. "I made some of those pants for her. They were tight at the waist, with zippers on both sides, and they zipped at the ankles. Muz said, 'When I have to go, I have to go!' She often wore a blue chambray shirt, like a man's. It was always buttoned up to the collar. Joe and Muz always did things together, but Muz didn't do a man's work like some women do now. Muz was always the hostess, and she was always feminine." That meant that Muz didn't work on engines, get greasy, or cut down trees. She added a soft touch to their homes, even the Reid Inlet cabin—window curtains, linens, flowers, and tidy gardens. She baked bread and pies, sent greeting cards to her friends, and wrote letters on flowered stationery.

"No matter how Muz felt the day you arrived," Nell said, "she always made you feel welcome. When Joe walked by Muz as they were working, he would give her a little tap on the head just to say hello. Muz was a name they made up. It was probably short for mother. Muz called him 'Daddy.' I think her real name was Shirley, but everyone called her Muz. As the Ibachs got older, Glen would tow a bulldozer across Icy Strait on a raft to haul logs for firewood from the beach, or to plow their garden, or do things Muz and Joe couldn't do any more.

"They grew great yellow Shasta daisies," Nell told me. "You could see their pansies from the water. One of their rooms was painted bright orange, with green on the molding and around the windows. It sounds like an awful combination, but Muz knew the value of bright color in this rainy country on dark days. That room was bright and felt warm and cozy no matter what the weather.

"They ate goose tongue from the beach," Nell remembered. "They put jars over dandelions to keep them clean. There weren't as many dandelions growing as there are now, of course. The Ibachs weren't ecologists, but if something was good they ate it. Once we ate fruitcake the Ibachs had kept for five years in a tin. The raisins had all gone to sugar, but it was so delicious. Muz put away all kinds of things here and there. One time she opened a jar, and we ate peacock tongues."

I imagine that the Ibachs ate well on Lemesurier, if the way people eat in Gustavus now is any indication. The Ibachs probably fished for halibut and salmon and no doubt hunted bear and deer. They would have dried and smoked the fish and the meat. They could dig for cockles and clams, gather mussels, and put out pots for crabs. They would gather strawberries, blueberries, and salmonberries. In the garden, they grew lettuce, carrots, peas, cabbage, beets, rutabagas, and potatoes, and stored their produce in a root cellar.

They would have bought flour, oatmeal, sugar, coffee and tea, raisins, chocolate, baking powder, yeast and canned milk in Juneau, and perhaps canned tomatoes, beans, and applesauce. They baked with eggs from their chickens, well fenced in to keep the foxes out.

"Joe would cook sourdoughs for breakfast, big thick ones," Nell remembered. "He was insulted if you didn't eat four or five. I could never eat that many. Sometimes Muz would serve me breakfast in bed, and she said she loved to do it."

Gustavus homesteaders worked hard. That was a necessity. The men, and some of the women, slogged through the mud, built houses, proved up on homesteads, fixed broken machines, dug for gold, and cut logs to build boats and bridges. That work was a source of pride. Still, it's not hard to imagine the pleasure for Nell of being served breakfast in bed—scrambled eggs and those pancakes, plus English black tea in china teacups and homemade bread with nagoonberry jam. As a young bride, it would be lovely to be pampered and mothered, a break from doing all the cooking and serving at home. It may have been like having a grown up daughter for Muz.

"The Ibachs made three fortunes," Nell told me. "One was in fox furs and one in gold. The other one I can't remember. They framed a large check, which they never cashed. It hung in their living room near the fireplace." In winter the Ibachs no doubt read by kerosene lamp. In summer it was light for hours. With the abundance of food and each other, what else could they possibly want? Money? They'd need a little. That's where raising foxes for pelts and gold mining came in.

"Joe was a big game hunter on Admiralty Island, as well as other places," Nell added. "Mining engineers came out all the time to look at his claims. Boatloads of people would stop at the Ibachs' place on Lemesurier. The Ibachs knew important people. Some of the people who stopped were invited, but many just came. Muz was famous for her dandelion wine. But after a few years, she stopped making it.

"Muz said, 'I want people to come to see *me*, not because of what I have.'" Nell told me that Muz Ibach never made dandelion wine after that.

I knew a few more details about the Ibachs and their lives after talking to Nell, but I still wasn't satisfied. She didn't provide the answer to my central question. I didn't yet know the essence of what was so special about the Ibachs.

"A year after Muz's death, Joe wrote me a letter," Nell said that afternoon before I left.

"'I'm not religious, but Muz was,' he wrote.

"I sent him an answer," Nell told me, "but it must have arrived in the mail just after he killed himself."

Joe had buried her in a mound of pansies.

IBACH HEADSTONE, WILLOUGHBY COVE, LEMESURIER ISLAND, APRIL 1999

Copyright Dave Bohn.

KEN YOUMANS
AND JOE IBACH,
LEMESURIER ISLAND,
OCTOBER 1954
Copyright Bruce Black.
Courtesy of Dave Bohn.

KEN YOUMANS

Most of the old-timers I interviewed in Gustavus were happy to share memories nonstop. Ken Youmans didn't fit the profile. For one thing, he was younger by ten or fifteen years than the people called old-timers back then. For another, he worked at the park, and there was a tangible but invisible line in those days between the park employees and homesteaders in Gustavus. It's a strange thing about human beings and their territories, one more way we are not so different from the other animals around us. (By the time Ken Youmans reached the "old-timer" stage, the phrase had mostly dropped from use, although you heard it occasionally.)

I arrived at the Youmans' house in Bartlett Cove at 7:00 p.m. as agreed. Ken opened the door and invited me in. His wife Ann was in the kitchen. She walked into the living room for a moment, said hello and disappeared. The one-story ranch house was built for year-round Park Service staff, the kind of house that would have fit into any U.S. suburb. Those houses always seemed out of place in the Glacier Bay landscape, although, painted gray with white trim, they blended into the forest and matched the color of the clouds. But those houses did have certain advantages—running water, indoor plumbing, oil heat, and washers and dryers. As maintenance foreman, Ken was responsible for their upkeep, along with the roads and water system and keeping bears away from the dump.

Ken sat in an easy chair. I sat on the couch. I turned on the tape recorder. I had let him know I was coming that night and what we would talk about, but up to that point I hadn't truly worked to create a rapport. That may explain why Ken's first answers were short and provided almost no information. It wasn't going to be an easy task, getting Ken Youmans to talk.

Usually, in an interview, I asked one or two questions and then sat back and listened. With Youmans, it was hard work. When I said, "So, you knew Muz and Joe Ibach?" he answered, "Yes, I did." I followed up with, "Did you know them well?" He said, "Yes, I knew them pretty well." I asked, "When did you meet them?" He replied, "About 1950, I guess."

It was going to be a long evening—one question from me and two or three words from Ken. Interviewing him was beginning to seem like using a shovel to dig into rock.

Maybe he, too, was uncomfortable, sitting there with the lengthening spaces in the conversation, or maybe it began to seem like a chance to tell stories to someone who would listen. Finally, at a point I think now was disconnected from anything I said or did, he started to give answers in whole sentences, and I didn't have to come up with so many questions.

He'd first come to Glacier Bay to work at the request of the superintendent for Glacier Bay National Monument, who was based in Sitka back then. Ken, who worked for the Territory of Alaska before the Park Service hired him, had already been coming to Glacier Bay on his summer vacations to "prospect around." He was hired as a seasonal ranger in Glacier Bay for the summer of 1949 and went back to Sitka in the fall. The Park Service offered him a permanent job as a ranger and then as a park historian, but he didn't want to do either. He finally accepted when they offered to hire him as the maintenance foreman.

"I haven't done anything but work here," he said. "Nothing exciting at all. It's just been one year after another, and they go along pretty fast."

I asked about mining in Glacier Bay. He said, "It's easy prospecting de-glaciated country, because there isn't much overburden. You can see all the rock formations. Everything's bare in Glacier Bay. Where the ice is retreating so fast, it's easy to determine what's there." Overburden is what miners call trees, plants, and topsoil, anything that covers up the ore and hides the veins. There was no soil or plant cover, and no trees in many parts of Glacier Bay when Joe Ibach and Ken Youmans prospected there. Prospecting wouldn't be easy now. In much of the upper bay, alders and willows cover the land.

Ken hadn't bothered to keep up his mining claims, to register them every year.

"Joe Ibach just kept his claims staked," Ken said. "As long as you staked them and put a notice on location markers, the claims were good for a year. I had my name on some of them. Joe told me, 'Why file? Once it's a matter of record, someone else can see where you are, and you're going to have people alongside of you.' I'd just re-stake them every year, and no one can jump your claim that way."

I asked if he thought Joe Ibach was satisfied.

"Well, he wanted to make money, and he made it all right, but he really enjoyed looking," Ken said. "Looking" meant prospecting. "He was a good geologist, and he found lots of things. He prospected in the Copper River Valley and some other areas, including Middleton Island. But miners find something and then they always want to go on and find something bigger, to look for the mother lode."

"Did he have everything he wanted?" I asked.

"Yes," Ken said, "I'm sure he did. I'm sure he was pretty well satisfied."

"Are there other people you can say that about?"

"Oh, I suppose so. I don't know right off hand," said Ken. "Joe had a nice place when he lived there. He had a world of friends."

KEN YOUMANS, 1989
Copyright Jim Mackovjak.

FOLLOWING THE TRAIL

October 1977. I was back on Bainbridge Island again. On a clear autumn day, I borrowed a friend's vintage 1949 Dodge truck, newly painted red, and drove it onto the ferry for the half hour ride to Seattle. I was taking supplies to Foss Tug to ship to Gustavus by barge: winter boots, jacket, raingear, canned tuna, and manual typewriter. The glaciers that once filled Puget Sound had been gone for ten thousand years, but signs of those glaciers were everywhere. I looked back at the island from the deck of the ferry and saw that glaciers had rounded those hills. The fog now rolled into Eagle Harbor in the same places that the ice once did.

My plan was to live in Gustavus with Fred that winter in his parents' cabin on the Salmon River flats. I drove the truck off the ferry in Seattle under the Alaskan Way viaduct and one block east to Western Ave. The day was warm for October. I wore brown high top boots, white carpenter's overalls, and a red wool shirt, a fashion statement for women on Bainbridge Island at the time. It was the second phase of the women's movement, and we wore clothes to indicate we were learning to do things we'd never done: play soccer, sail boats and fix cars.

On the right, at the corner of Madison and First, I saw the sign for Turner and Pease, a wholesale distributor of cheese, butter, and eggs. I'd forgotten to get directions to the Foss Tug office in West Seattle to ship my supplies to the Gustavus dock. It was long before the days of the Internet, mobile phones and GPS. I parked the truck and walked into Turner and Pease to use their telephone book.

I leaned my elbows on their counter and saw cheese in a refrigerated case. Blocks of cheddar encased in wax. Cheese would keep on the long journey up the Inside Passage, so I might as well order some, I thought. I stood in the entry next to a small office of metal desks and paper invoices waiting for my will call order. The man behind the counter was used to large wholesale orders, no doubt, not a request for five blocks of cheddar, but he was polite. Pointing out the front window at the bright red truck loaded with boxes of supplies, another man in the office looked at me and asked, "Where are you shipping all that?" Normal curiosity, I supposed, his break from the daily routine.

"To Alaska. Glacier Bay," I said.

A third man sat at the back of the office, far away from the windows and light. Medium height, stocky build, gray hair, his back was turned toward me. He swiveled his chair around and said, "Glacier Bay. I've been there." On a cruise ship, I imagined.

I expected the story of his cruise ship voyage with his wife. That would be usual. But then came the kind of miracle that happens if you listen to your intuition when it says, "You need directions to West Seattle. You might as well stay to buy cheese."

"Some friends and I mined for gold in a place called Reid Inlet," he said. "We worked for a man named Joe Ibach."

Too shocked to ask questions, I took the cheese and said, "Okay if I come back to talk?" and he answered, "Yes."

SCABIES

I shipped the supplies from Seattle by barge, and Fred picked them up at the dock. Fred and I lived in his family's cabin that fall after his parents went south. They had built the cabin on a bank in a curve of the Salmon River, in a meadow on the flats. We pumped water by hand and heated it on the oil stove. The town had ninety-three registered voters. Most people left for the winter. In Gustavus, I wasn't alone, but living there, near the four corners, where the two main roads meet, I still felt isolated. Most of the houses and cabins were hidden in the woods. There was almost nothing to see from the road in the "center of town" except the Gustavus Inn on one side with Henrietta's place nearby; Jack and Sally Lesh's cabin on the riverbank in the meadow near the bridge with the Howes' cabin behind it; the old Matson house across the river; and a few cabins hidden in the trees.

One day, when the weather was cloudy but dry, wind calm, and the tide right, Fred and I motored in his fishing boat, the *Amalie L*, to the house where the Ibachs once lived on Lemesurier Island across Icy Strait.

Fred anchored the boat, and we rowed to shore and walked up the path. A bearskin rug hung on the living room wall, back paws reaching up to the ceiling, head and front paws on the floor. I saw the room Muz painted orange and green to keep their spirits up during short winter days and gray skies. I read a note in the guest log written when Muz and Joe were gone.

"We helped ourselves to vegetables from the garden," said the note, "as you instructed."

I love reading books about places I know, connecting the story and land. That didn't happen much for me in Missouri, unless you count *The Adventures of Huckleberry Finn* and *Tom Sawyer*. T.S. Eliot wrote "The Waste Land" in England, long after he left St. Louis. There's something different about reading a book that takes place where you live.

I took home to Gustavus from the Ibachs' library a children's book called *The Pirates of Icy Strait*, about pirates who stole salmon from local fish traps and a boy who helped capture the pirates in Taylor Bay near the Brady Glacier. I liked the story of the pirates and fish traps and the local place names. I think Gustavus homesteaders Nell and Glen

Parker gave the Ibachs that book. Part of the story took place in Excursion Inlet and some of it on Lemesurier. The next spring, Fred returned the book on his way to Inian Island to go fishing. Fred returned it because that's what you did in Alaska, where you couldn't easily replace what you owned and where even a single book was precious. I didn't want to treat that book as I often did, borrow it and forget to return it. I had taken it to read; no one had given it to me as a gift. I wanted to treat it with reverence. Even though the Ibachs were dead, it seemed to me that keeping the book would be a breach of a trust with them.

The previous summer I had lived at the Inian Island homestead for three months. I thought I would live forever on that island with Fred in a two-story green wood house with a garden, a greenhouse, a dock, and a big building stuffed with tools and parts that they called the warehouse. The other inhabitants of the homestead were fishermen in their twenties and thirties, mostly men, plus a couple of women.

I knew from *The Land and the Silence* that Joe and Muz had lived for a time on a windswept island in the Gulf of Alaska one hundred and seventy-three miles south of Anchorage, near Prince William Sound. They raised blue foxes for pelts, as they did on Lemesurier. Foxes couldn't escape from an island, although they disappeared into the Lemesurier woods.

Did I want to be like the Ibachs? Quite likely, but I didn't know it. I am sure that Fred didn't know I was attempting to live a storybook island life. I wanted to be happy like the Ibachs. I thought that Inian Island would be the perfect place to write.

I was waiting for inspiration. Every day I slept late. I neglected the garden and greenhouse. I didn't even cook.

"I am writing," I said, but I wasn't. I didn't help with the work. I didn't clean fish, although I was happy to eat fresh salmon and halibut that the fishermen caught.

That was the summer of a scabies epidemic among Southeast Alaska fishermen. I heard about it through the fishermen's grapevine, probably from one of the roving clan of fishermen who anchored at the Inian Island homestead. I didn't pay much attention.

What could that have to do with me? I noticed bumps and blisters and relentless itching and went to see the public health nurse who stopped periodically in Elfin Cove. Scabies are parasites. They have eight legs, so they're not insects, and they can't be seen with the naked eye. They crawl but cannot fly or jump. They burrow into skin.

The nurse listened to my complaint, severe itching that got worse at night. She inspected my body and said that scabies are transmitted by skin-to-skin contact. She told me that scabies were the seven-year itch in the Bible.

"Who do you sleep with?" she asked. That did it. Her diagnosis must be wrong. I couldn't possibly have a disease like that.

By the time I was willing to admit that the nurse was right, it was November, Fred and I were living in Gustavus, and the scabies had dug in. The itching was unceasing. I don't know how I got scabies, which can infest a host with no sign for two months. But Fred got them from me, and the itching got worse. We had to do something.

Fred went to Juneau by small plane to get medication at the public health service. The medication was scarce, and the health service was running out. They gave us one bottle of medication for the two of us. We didn't tell anyone.

The treatment required washing all our clothes, blankets and sheets, taking baths, slathering on medication, and doing it again the next day. Scabies are highly contagious.

We had no running water. We pumped water by hand. We heated that water and washed our clothes, including wool pants and sweaters. We hung the clothes outside on the line where they froze in bizarre shapes in below-freezing weather. This was a usual method for drying clothes in winter: you took a stick or a broom and knocked the ice out of them once the clothes were frozen. My Irish fisherman's sweater turned pink in spots from the hand spun, hand-dyed socks I washed with it, so I dyed that sweater the carmine color that comes from cochineal, little Mexican bugs. I poured the vermilion dye bath onto snow.

Fred pumped water from a red iron hand pump in the kitchen sink and carried it outside to fill the hot tub in the field, a metal horse-watering trough. We built a fire in the Japanese boiler and added wood all day till the water was hot. Then we sat in the hot tub and watched as the sky bathed itself in a shower of sparks from the wood stove, near snow that had turned the deep red color of the aurora borealis.

Though the scene was beautiful and poetic, a body covered with itching sores didn't fulfill my idea of a romantic life in Alaska. I lasted two months. The day after Christmas, I flew south to Seattle and the land of the laundromats.

The next summer I told Carol Janda about having scabies. The Jandas lived in Park Service housing. Bartlett Cove had its own generator for electricity and hot running water.

Carol said, "You should have come to the park and used our washer and dryer."

In those years, Ken Youmans' daughter Aimee lived across the Salmon River with a clear view of our place. Her family had bought Ruth and Fred Matson's old homestead when the Matsons moved to Sitka to live in the Pioneer Home. Aimee's father worked at the park when Fred's father was the park superintendent. Aimee had known Fred for a long time. She could see the Howes' cabin from her front window. In the years before Gustavus had electricity, for Aimee, watching any action across the river outside of our cabin on the flats must have been the equivalent of watching television.

Thirty-six years later in Aimee's kitchen over a cup of mint tea, I mentioned our bout with scabies.

Aimee said, "I always wondered why the two of you did so much laundry."

GEORGE SHURIN

I had thought I would live in Alaska forever. I thought I would live with Fred. I hadn't stayed one winter. In January 1977, I was back on Bainbridge Island again. What to do next? By spring I found my bearings. I wasn't living in Alaska, but I could write about it.

A couple of months later, in March, I took the ferry to Seattle and walked across the Madison Street pedestrian bridge over Harbor Way and under the Alaskan Way viaduct, down the metal stairs and through the door of Turner and Pease. I found George Shurin, the former miner who worked with Joe Ibach. He told me a story.

"In the fall of 1946, Joe came down with appendicitis. Muz built a great big bonfire on the beach at Lemesurier, because they had no other communication with the outside world. She stoked that fire for eighteen or twenty-four hours until a fishing boat recognized the SOS signal.

"They took Joe to the hospital in Juneau, but Muz wouldn't go to town. Radio stations were the main source of information. Muz turned on the Juneau radio station every afternoon, and they'd announce Joe's condition in the hospital.

"I think Muz Ibach was a chorus girl," Shurin told me. He met Joe only once. The Ibachs didn't come to Reid Inlet the summer that Shurin worked there.

"My brother knew them better," he said.

"Where does your brother live?"

"Royal City, Washington."

"How can I get in touch with him?"

"I haven't heard from him in a while." Shurin couldn't give me a phone number or address.

His brother's name was Mike Seiler. Maybe I could find Mike. I was still looking for an answer to my question: "What was so special about the Ibachs?"

SEA LIONS, POINT CAROLUS, 2006

Copyright Fritz Koschmann.

RADIO WAVES

April 1978. In my friend Megan's mauve-colored Mazda station wagon, I drove alone from Seattle due east. The high plateau of central Washington State was a blaze of spring wildflowers. East of Ellensburg, I crossed the river. The Columbia at that point flows south from its headwaters in Canada, before the Snake joins it and the Columbia turns west to form the boundary between Washington and Oregon.

I didn't know how to find Mike Seiler, but I had lived on Bainbridge Island and in Gustavus. I knew you could find people in small towns. You just asked people, because they knew everyone else, or you asked the universe to have them show up.

In the 1970s in Gustavus, the postmaster was Archie Chase's son Gene. During the fall and winter, a mail plane came in three times a week as long as the weather permitted. In summer, the protocol for visitors was to let Gene know, and he'd hold mail general delivery. In the long days of summer, when the fishermen were out on the water until dusk, at about 11:00 p.m., they would drive to Gene's house at midnight and wake him up to mail a letter. Gene finally gave instructions to drop off mail at the post office entrance after it closed. In the morning, he'd add the required number of stamps and run a tab for the sender.

My first summer in Alaska, I made a friend who worked for the Park Service in Bartlett Cove. Neither of us had a telephone, when landlines were the only option. It seemed to me that the airwaves were clearer in Glacier Bay. More than once over the summer, I would think of Patty in her trailer at the park headquarters, hoping to see her that evening. Then, like a receiver responding to a radio wave, as if I had sent a signal, within a few hours, she'd show up: "I've been thinking of you. What a beautiful evening! Do you have time to go for a walk?"

That September I went to Anchorage, where Patty had moved for the winter. I had an address but no phone number for her, and I wanted to see her. I got on a bus one morning without knowing if she would be home. I got off of the bus at the stop near her house just as Patty was ready to step on.

In that pure Alaska air, meetings happened that way again and again. Perhaps it was because of the absence of radio waves and of other kinds of interference that Patty and I tuned in to a frequency that seemed to exist beyond usual human sensing. It happened to me often in Alaska, with few telephones, few microwaves, and few people. But it is just as likely that what was clearer in Alaska was my brain.

Back in Royal City, Washington, that spring day, I pulled into the parking lot of the low-rise PUD building, the Public Utility District. Inside, a woman stood behind the counter. Her gray hair was pulled back from her face.

"How can I help you?" she asked.

"I'm looking for a man named Mike Seiler," I said. "I don't have his address." Royal City was a small town. In 2010, the population was just over two thousand people, and no doubt it was smaller when I went. The woman looked in a file, made notes with a pen, and then handed me a piece of paper, saying, "Is this who you're looking for?"

She had written a street name and number on it without asking why I wanted to find him.

LETTER FROM JOE
IBACH TO JACK AND
SHIRLEY CALLAHAN,
JUNE 1, 1959
*Courtesy of
John D. Feagin Sr.*

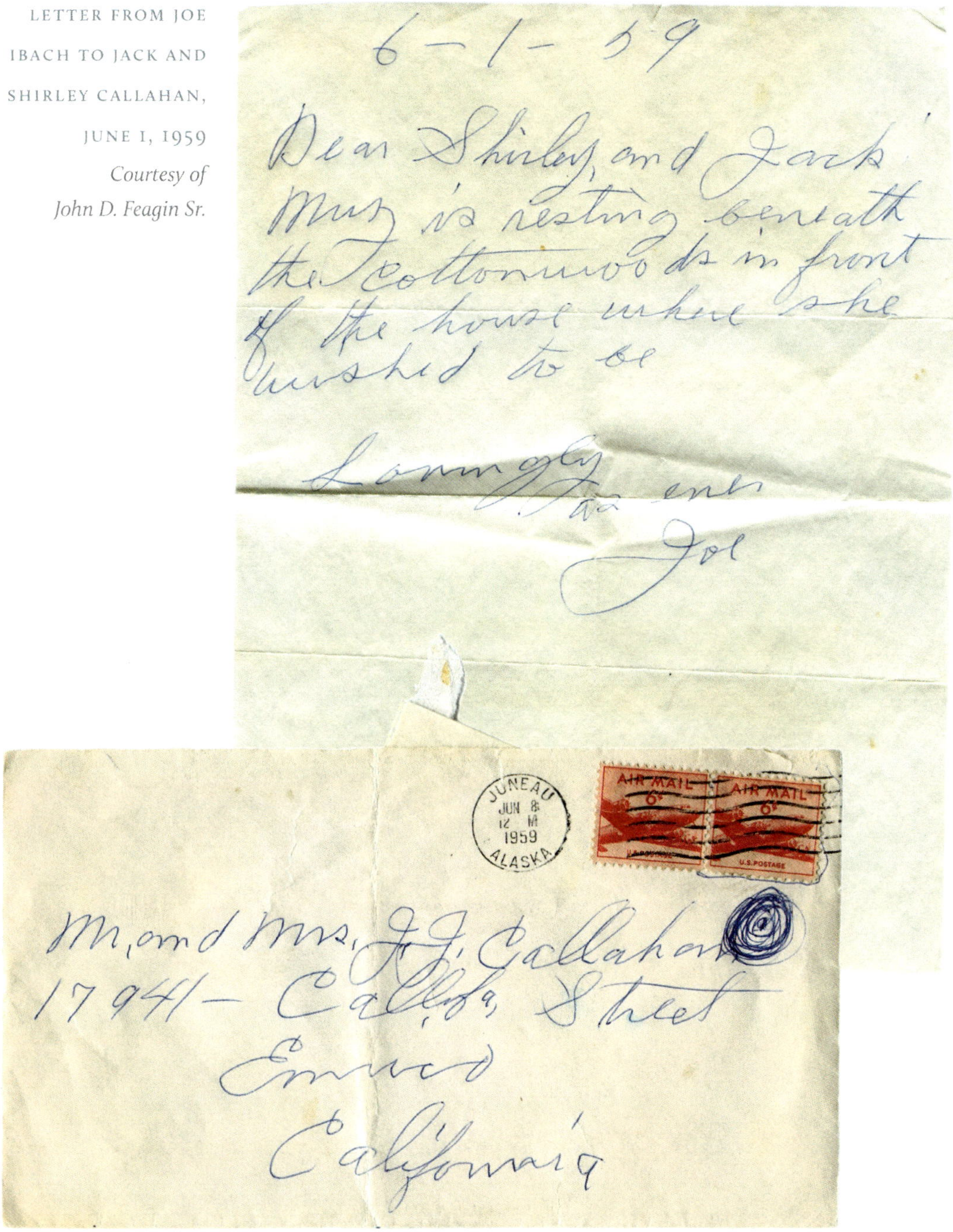

> 6-1-59
>
> Dear Shirley and Jack,
>
> Muz is resting beneath the cottonwoods in front of the house where she wished to be
>
> Lovingly for ever
>
> Joe

Mr. and Mrs. J. J. Callahan
1794 — Calif. Street
Emwood
California

EVERYTHING THEY WANTED

WILLIAM O. FIELD AND DAVE BOHN, HUGH MILLER INLET, SEPTEMBER 1966
Photograph by Lynn Kinsman. Courtesy of Dave Bohn.

MIKE SEILER

Mike Seiler's trailer sat on a small piece of land on a street lined with trees. It wasn't a mobile home park, more like a street with pre-fab homes. I knocked on the door. A stocky man wearing a gray shirt and who looked like he was in his sixties said, yes, he was Mike Seiler, he was busy, and could I come back tomorrow? Passing him on the street in Seattle, I would have walked by without thinking twice.

Perhaps Mike had plans for the day or didn't want his silence interrupted. I was on my way to Coulee Dam, one hundred and twelve miles north, to see Chuck and Carol Janda, who had moved there from Bartlett Cove. I told Mike I didn't have much time if I was going to make it to Coulee Dam by dark. I was half way down the thirty-foot long concrete walkway to the street when I heard him say: "Well, on second thought, why don't you come in?"

We sat across from each other in armchairs.

"What do you want to know?" he asked

"Tell me about the Ibachs," I said, although I had left my tape recorder in the car. *If I go out to get it,* I thought, *he'll remember that he was busy, and he won't tell me everything I want to hear.* Mike had already started talking, and I didn't want to stop him.

The blazing sun of a desert afternoon streamed in through the window. He didn't act like a host. He didn't offer me water or tea, but I hadn't come for that. I sat there with my notebook and pen and started writing as fast as I could. Mike started out in a formal tone.

"I met Muz and Joe about 1940, I guess," he said. "They were two of a kind. I don't suppose you'll ever find two like them. It's hard to say why you like one person and not another, but they had an aura. You wouldn't forget them if you met them once."

"Okay," I wondered, "but why?" I leaned further forward in my chair, but I didn't interrupt. I hunched over pencil and pad. I looked out the window. A few clouds floated in a clear sky.

I didn't arrive with a list of questions. What can be learned from a place like this? It was a hard question to answer directly. I liked to start an interview with the basics, for example, "When did you first come here?" and then see what people said. Usually they answered with surface details, but, along the way, they dug deeper. At the end of an interview a person might come to an awareness they hadn't put into words.

"I don't think Muz and Joe treated anyone differently whether the people came in a skiff or on a hundred-foot schooner," Mike said. "The two of them were very kind. A lot of important people visited them. They made other people feel better. Of course, a lot of people took advantage. I don't know how people found out, but they'd all come to visit Joe and Muz. Their hospitality and their generosity were wonderful." Mike was looking past me as he spoke. In his way, he was generous, too.

"Muz's parents were owners of a small hotel and restaurant in New York City. She gave me a set of dishes from that restaurant. Joe met her on one of his visits to New York," said Mike. "She and Joe spoke with words from back east, words we never used out here."

I wish I'd asked Mike what words they used. When Mike said, "They were not the kind to show everything they knew, unless you'd been there for a while and got to know them," I imagined this was also true of Mike.

"The two of them were quite learned," Mike continued. "They read a lot, like most Alaskans at that time." I knew the Ibachs rubbed elbows with celebrities and that John Barrymore had been their houseguest. Barrymore's bathtub can still be found near the Lemesurier house. Linda Parker, Gustavus historian and daughter-in-law of Glen Parker's older brother Les, told me years later that the Ibachs were more elegant than most local homesteaders, and yet they were entirely down to earth.

Linda said, "They had the kind of touch that put everyone, wealthy or poor in terms of the world's goods, at ease. They never put themselves above anyone else." I have met Tlingit elders who had this ability, along with a self-deprecating sense of humor. I think that humor and humility are two characteristics of the best people in any culture.

"The Ibachs lived pretty much on the land," Mike told me. "Muz canned a tremendous amount of fish and other seafood, and Joe raised a large garden. With the fish and the garden and the deer and the bear, they were able to sustain themselves until they were real old."

I sat still. I didn't move.

"I think that the first worries of their life came when they got old," Mike continued. "You know, when you're young, you never know what it's going to feel like to be old. Muz died first, from cancer. I think it was because of the hard work. That little woman worked like a beaver. Joe did the hunting, but she did all the rest. She would carry the meat down. The skin of a bear is real heavy. I think her injuries from that work were her undoing. And then Joe being alone there… Of course, Joe didn't mind being alone, but being entirely alone…"

The sun was lower in the sky. Big clouds gathered in the dry air outside, east of the Cascade Mountains. I wasn't going to tell him to stop. I didn't ask for a drink or a snack. I wasn't thirsty or hungry because I was swept away by the stories.

Mike told this story about Muz: "About a half mile from their place on Lemesurier, there was a very white calcite rock, pure white. One year, about 1941, Muz decided she wanted that white calcite brought down to make a walkway. So she brought down the rock and floated it up the beach, sack by sack. There must have been hundreds of sacks. In front of the house, the walk was one hundred feet long. Along the side of the house it was about thirty feet, and there were two other walks. Almost every year, as long as she was able, she put the rock in tubs with soap of some kind and washed it and put it all down again in the walk." In that rainy country, moss would grow. You could slip on slimy green rock.

I sat in my chair and kept writing. I wrote fast to capture the flow and intonation of Mike's way of speaking. I wrote in the tiniest possible script so I wouldn't run out of paper. (I was the kind of note-taker in college who wrote down by hand every word.

Then, when it came time to take a test, the ideas just came out of my hand. Were the ideas mine? No, they weren't, but I didn't care about that. Give the professor what he wanted. That was my intent. See it all for myself? Until I met the independent people of Bartlett Cove and Gustavus, it never occurred to me that I could follow my own path or have my own way of looking at the world.)

"Muz put in a garden every year. Hers were the flowers, and she was a personal friend of every one. His were the vegetables. I don't think she cared as much for the gold, but it was Joe's life. She didn't give a hoot about it. But what excited him excited her.

"In the fall, when the wind started to blow, there would be tons of kelp piled up on the beach. They'd have a pile of it over fifteen feet high and use it for fertilizer. It would lie in the sun and get hot and be full of flies and worms. The flies and worms would digest it down to a foot, and that was their fertilizer. Half the island was limestone and the other half acid, so that provided acid and sweetener. They grew a good garden." I had read about that garden in their guestbook, when Fred and I went across Icy Strait on his boat on a fall day trip from Gustavus to Lemesurier.

"Joe had his own still, you know, back in the woods," Mike said. "He loved to get people drunk. He was always concocting a new mixture—black currants, red currants, mushrooms, bark in it—he'd try anything. He'd have you drunk in nothing flat. Some of that stuff was dynamite. Muz didn't really like to partake. She would take a little sip, just to try it." I could picture that, Muz smiling at Joe, wearing the special pants she asked Nell Parker to make and a buttoned up blue Chambray shirt.

"Muz was very small. She came from New York, like Joe did," Mike said. (Although Muz and Joe met in New York, Muz was born in Canada.)

"Joe was a very hard worker, a pleasant man, too, and he did the guiding, but a lot of the work was left to Muz." It was getting late in the afternoon. I could see through the window the light fading. But I didn't move in the chair. I didn't know what time it was, I didn't look at my watch, and Mike kept talking.

"I guess you know they had a house in Glacier Bay at Reid Inlet. I lived in it one year," Mike said. "They planted the strawberries that grew there. They used to anchor a boat in the little pond." That land has risen approximately three centimeters a year since Joe died in 1960.

"You'd hear the glacier continually," Mike said. "It was only about half a mile away from the cabin when I lived there, and it kept going back." When I first saw the Ibachs' cabin in Reid Inlet in 1976, the glacier was three miles in the distance.

I envied Mike when he told me that. The Ibachs must have trusted him, to let him live in their cabin when they were gone. Mike said a year, but that most likely meant a summer. Did he live in the Reid Inlet cabin in the winter? Probably he didn't.

I was listening for stories that would provide the details of the Ibachs' lives and the answers to what they were like. Mike talked about more than simply details. I listened harder, and I kept writing, even after my fingers got stiff and my wrist began to hurt. I sat and wrote as the light changed and afternoon turned to dusk. I paused to look out at the pale pink sky, at the fading light. Mike talked about Muz and Joe Ibach, and he talked for three hours.

"You might say they enjoyed life—lived close to nature," Mike said, "but the time came when they couldn't cope with it. In spite of all the friends they had, well, old Father Time came along, and that's it."

I wasn't sure what I was seeking on that drive to Royal City, except to find Mike. Some intuition said, "Go!" That day I felt a connection to this man I didn't know and would never see again, because we loved the same people, Muz and Joe Ibach, and the same place, Reid Inlet. Of course, I had never met the Ibachs in person, and Mike Seiler had. I felt sad: a feeling of longing for something missed or lost. Mike's face didn't change, but he looked away. I am good at picking up other people's emotions. Maybe that feeling of longing was mine, or maybe it belonged to us both.

"Being independent like they had, I think they were philosophically prepared for death, but I don't think they were any way prepared that it would come so soon," Mike said. "It was kind of a calamitous death. I should have been there, I suppose." He looked into the distance. "But you know, you have your own things to do. I was mining somewhere else at the time—seven days a week, fourteen hours a day. It was hard to get away. We wrote, and we had lots of dreams, things we were going to do together, and it never got done." I heard Mike's regret: the young man, alone, focused on his work and perhaps not so good at relationships, a man who, like most of us, doesn't realize how quickly things alter. Mike's brother George said that the Ibachs treated Mike like a son.

Mike's voice got quiet when he talked about their deaths, and I could sense his sadness. He didn't mention that Joe Ibach died from a self-inflicted gunshot wound in 1960, the year after Muz died, although he skirted around it. Mike would have known that I knew of the suicide pact and that Joe had kept the promise. Everyone who knew about the Ibachs knew that, so Mike didn't have to say it. The Ibachs had lived together all that time, with visitors but otherwise alone. It was clear they completely loved each other. With a deep connection like that, I understood the desire not to live on.

I didn't ask Mike if he'd talked with Muz and Joe about their idea that one would die if the other did, or whose idea that suicide pact was. I didn't know Mike well enough, and I wasn't an investigator or detective. Mike's circumvention was something to honor. It seemed intrusive to ask.

Now, thinking it over, I imagine the idea was Joe's. If Joe had died first, I think that Muz would have lived.

"Muz was about five-two," Mike said. "Joe was taller, but not six feet. He was built like rawhide—tough and lean. He was a talker. She was quiet." And then Mike paused.

"As for which of them was the stronger, I couldn't say," he said. "But I think she was."

When Mike said he thought Muz was the stronger of the two, I knew I had come for this.

I didn't ask Mike why he said Muz was stronger than Joe. He may have meant physical strength. But I think he meant emotionally. I think he meant strength in spirit. I didn't know the Ibachs. I didn't know Mike well. But the essence of what he said rang true. I was under the spell of the story. What he said was enough.

I was longing for a sense in my life that came from the strength of feminine presence. Seeing it in other women is one way a woman can find her own strength. If other women have found it, she, too, can find it within herself. In a time when men still seemed to order the world, I hadn't yet seen my own mother's strength, as I saw it on the day she died. I didn't know that my real question was: "How do I be a woman?" To become a woman is not simply a physical process.

"Do you want to see my Glacier Bay rocks?" Mike asked me as the sun was setting.

"Yes," I said. He stood up.

Dr. William Osgood Field, the glaciologist who studied Glacier Bay beginning in 1926, kept files of photographs of glaciers in various stages of retreat and advance, in tall cabinets in his New York office on Park Avenue in the Sherry Netherland Hotel. Mike Seiler was a miner. In his trailer in Royal City, Washington, he had a closet full of rocks from the places he'd worked in Alaska and the western U.S.

Mike opened the door of the closet and pulled out a cardboard box. In it lay a large piece of white calcite rock from Lemesurier Island plus five or six small rocks from Reid Inlet.

I didn't ask Mike how many times he'd moved those rocks linked to a place and two people he loved. A single rock is likely to weigh more than photographs, although, with the number of photographs Bill Field took, his photographs no doubt weighed more.

When the interview with Mike was over, I walked out into dry desert air. It was evening. I had only asked one or two questions. Mike answered the questions I didn't know to ask.

Was Joe Ibach satisfied? Did he have everything he wanted? I didn't ask Mike straight out, but it didn't seem to matter. Mike's trailer house was the place where the vein got rich, and I found the mother lode, as Ptarmigan Creek miner Leslie Parker would have said. Finding it, I was satisfied. I had found what I needed about the Ibachs. It wasn't just that they loved each other. It was this: of the two, Muz was stronger.

I never saw Mike Seiler after that day. I haven't gone back to Royal City. Mike was part of a community of people who crossed paths in Reid Inlet once upon a time and who lived in my imagination. It wasn't simply that he offered a way to know how life was in and around Glacier Bay in the 1940s and 50s. His life sounded hard and lonely, and I wouldn't want to live it. I don't think I would have spent much time with Mike if I had lived down the street from him. But in telling me about the Ibachs, he became a source of my strength, although I was a miner who followed the veins of human stories into the depths. I had listened to intuition and found him. I was beginning to trust myself.

I stopped for gas in Royal City, because I didn't know if a gas station would be open late at night on the road to Coulee Dam one hundred miles away. I pulled up to the pump, filled the tank, and then discovered that I had left my glasses at Mike's house. Without them I wouldn't be able to see well enough to drive on two-lane back roads in the dark.

And besides, I'd given Mike no gift, except, perhaps, that I listened. I wasn't very wise about honoring people then, but I knew I'd left something unfinished. I recognized the sign. Forgetting my glasses meant that I hadn't quite been ready to leave his house. I drove back under dark clouds.

My glasses were on Mike's living room table. From the trunk of my friend Megan's car, I pulled out a typed copy of poems I'd written about Reid Inlet and Joe and Muz Ibach, and I gave the poems to Mike. I carried poems of Reid Inlet with me the way Dr. Field stored photographs of the glaciers and the way Mike Seiler carried rocks.

"May I use your name in this book?" I asked Mike.

"It's okay," he said. "I don't deserve it, but if you want to, okay. It takes two or three times for a person to remember me, but Muz and Joe had an aura. You wouldn't forget them if you met them one time. I haven't done anything special. I was just born, raised, and tried to live.

"Don't work too hard on your writing," he said. "Wherever you are, live life. Enjoy it like Muz and Joe."

That's the gospel according to Mike Seiler. The earth speaks with human lips.

DRYAS SEEDS, 2004
Copyright Sean Neilson.

TRANSFORMATION

Snow falls in high elevations and accumulates layer upon layer. Winter after winter, it builds. The weight of snow on top compresses and transforms the layers of ice underneath. Over time, under pressure, the crystals beneath change into a different form and structure. Through heat generated by the upper layers, the crystalline structure of the ice below undergoes a metamorphosis. I read this in a geology text I found on a university library shelf.

I read that geologists categorize rock in three ways: igneous, with exposure to fire; sedimentary, in layers of deposits; and metamorphic, formed when deposits on top create pressure, causing the crystalline structure of rock to change shape: granite to gneiss; and schist from shale, basalt and slate. I also read that geologists categorize glacial ice as a form of metamorphic rock. I wondered how this could be.

I asked park research biologist Greg Streveler about how ice can be considered rock. Streveler, as knowledgeable about the Bay as perhaps anyone living, gave me this explanation: "Rock is solid at normal temperatures, and water is liquid. But rock becomes liquid at very high heat, and water, when frozen, is solid. Thus the states of water and rock are a function of temperature; ice and rock change state in this fashion. Because of this similarity, geologists consider that glacial ice is a form of metamorphic rock." His statement, to me, is not so different from poetry.

Chuck Jurasz, who taught high school science in Juneau and spent summers studying humpback whales, tells me this years later, as we sit on the deck outside my home in Oregon and hear the sound of cars, not of glaciers: "The way snow becomes ice is not unlike the way the weight of sediment forms sand into sandstone. In the same process, discarded shells from billions of sea creatures become limestone on the sea floor. At first, the rock is like eggs in a pan, loose and flowing. With heat, it congeals or sets, the same way that the elements of concrete set when you add water to them." He is good at explanations.

"In a similar way, snow squeezes itself to make glacial ice," Chuck continues. "Snow will collapse, that is, avalanche, the way solids collapse in a rockslide. Only when snow becomes glacial ice, under pressure, does it flow."

Chuck says, "In a next step, when weight increases from more layers on top, limestone, squeezed, becomes marble. That's how the Marble Islands in Glacier Bay were formed." I've seen birds nesting on the Marble Islands over forty years and sea lions resting at their base but never asked how that rock took shape.

Chuck continues: "When tectonic plates and continents meet, one sliding beneath another, the land is pushed up along with limestone or marble on the seabed. That uplift is the process that makes mountains. Although building mountains takes thousands of years, glaciers form in a couple of hundred. Human beings can directly see that process of glacier formation." Chuck is seventy-six, but his voice is the same as at age thirty-nine when I first interviewed him.

He says, "Most sedimentation in Glacier Bay is the result of glacial activity. Ice is the most fragile of rocks, but, in mass, it gouges rock out. Glacial ice shapes the rock beneath like a bowl. Glaciers also carry broken-off rock on top. Then rivers formed from glacial melt water sort out the smaller rocks and gravel. The streams drop heavy gravel first.

"What's left," he continues, "on the floor of the fjords are super-fine clays. Those clays polish the sea bottom. There isn't much on the sea bottom to refract sound. It travels underwater there for a long time. The smoothness of those fjords in Glacier Bay and their shape is one reason that underwater sound in Glacier Bay is so problematic for whales." Chuck's days of leaping into boats are over. He looks older, as do we all. But he is still curious about everything, and he looks out from the same clear eyes.

Because Chuck says this, I picture how fine glacial till shaved off from the mountainsides polishes that underwater rock smooth. I imagine the bowl in which a whale swims; that it lives in a world of water where sound flows through the current. I imagine what it is to be a whale, as Chuck did years ago, and I think of my own sensitivity to sound, how I suffered in noise-filled cities before I thought to carry earplugs. This is how geology—ice, water and rock—shape the whales' lives as well as ours.

Imagining all this isn't so hard, once I get the hang of it, as Carolyn Elder, a Glacier Bay naturalist, wrote in her small book, "Hiking Guide to Muir Inlet," May 1975, first edition. She never wrote a second. The alders grew up so thick and fast in Muir Inlet that you couldn't hike cross-country anymore in the places about which she wrote. No point in revising the guide.

In ordinary reality, when we look at rock, it appears to be solid and concrete. Rock, and everything else in the world, is whole and complete in each instant, although from moment to moment, things shift. This basic concept is evoked in many categories of thinking: geology, archaeology, philosophy, poetry, in the worldview of many indigenous peoples, and in the visions of religious mystics. Ice, rock, grass-of-Parnassus, lichens, mud, and our own bodies exist in a state of temporary wholeness in a total sea of being. For me, the earth is like water, in this sense, that it rarely holds still. Whales sing in a fluid, ever-changing space. Perhaps we human beings will be able to see enough aspects of our world as it changes itself, and as we change it, to imagine ourselves into new modes of seeing, to evolve, to expand into new ways of being. Perhaps our minds will do this as well: collect facts and experiences until, under pressure, we come to see the world in a new way, and we act from that different awareness.

"Reid Glacier's ice doesn't have the usual cloudy-white appearance that most glaciers have," Chuck tells me. "The deep blue of Reid's ice argues for a long, slow transformation, that gases including oxygen were driven out of it over a long period of time. That ice is transparent, not simply translucent. You can see through Reid Glacier's ice."

I see this: Chuck has put his whole energy into these descriptions, as he always did, so that I will understand. He used a similar process, I think, to imagine what life was like for whales. It's the difference between saying the words of a song and singing it. To see the story of how things are created and shaped, to see what other people have not seen, you have to love yourself into it, I think—to use every element of your being, not simply observe, detached, from outside. Many Glacier Bay scientists do this.

Plato, quoting Pythagoras, once wrote that stone is frozen music.

DOC G.

I met Dr. Richard P. Goldthwait in 1979, the one hundredth anniversary of John Muir's first Glacier Bay visit. John Muir came to Glacier Bay in the 1800s because he wanted to witness in present time the way that ice shapes the land. His intention was to see a living glacial landscape to confirm his theory that glaciers carved Yosemite Valley. He succeeded.

Dr. Goldthwait first came to Glacier Bay's outer coast as a Dartmouth student, part of the "Harvard-Dartmouth Expeditions" organized by Bradford Washburn in 1933 and '34. Bradford Washburn is known for the first aerial mapping and photography of the world's mountains, including Denali and the Himalayas. Washburn and Goldthwait met originally as captains of their respective college sports teams, Goldthwait at Dartmouth and Washburn at Harvard. In 1934, members of their Harvard-Dartmouth expedition climbed 12,728 ft. Mt. Crillon on Glacier Bay's outer coast.

Mike Seiler told me a story about Barbara Washburn, who climbed with her husband. In 1940, before crossing the Brady ice field on their way to the top of Mt. Bertha, the Washburns stayed in Reid Inlet with Muz and Joe Ibach. (Barbara Washburn was the first woman to climb Mt. McKinley, now called Denali, in 1947.)

A flock of ravens frequented the Ibachs' cabin. One day Barbara Washburn hung her bright-colored laundry outside it to dry. (A flock of crows is called a murder. A flock of ravens is called a parliament, a conspiracy, or an unkindness. As a group, they are known to taunt predators.)

Mesmerized by the colors, those ravens made off with what Mike Seiler called "that woman's galore of washing." Years later, Barbara Washburn told me that she was pregnant the day they climbed Mt. Bertha. While climbing, she ate only a handful of pilot crackers.

After World War II ended, Dr. Goldthwait returned with Dr. William O. Field on a tour of Glacier Bay's inside waters. During his career, Field measured the advance and retreat of the glaciers in the bay over a span of more than fifty years. He first came to

BARBARA WASHBURN DESCENDING FIRST FEW STEPS OF MOUNT BERTHA,
GLACIER BAY NATIONAL MONUMENT,
ALASKA, 1940

Copyright Bradford Washburn. Courtesy of DecaneasArchive.com.

Glacier Bay when he was a Harvard student in 1926. With Field, Goldthwait toured the bay, making a list of all the geology and glaciology research questions they could think of. In 1960, Goldthwait helped form the Institute of Polar Studies, now called the Byrd Polar and Climate Research Center, at The Ohio State University. Over the years, Goldthwait crossed each question off the list as he assigned these studies to PhD students who came to his office in search of dissertation topics.

Goldthwait was probably five feet seven inches in height. His solid body and confident personality seemed right for a geologist. His hair was dark with silver streaks. Generations of students called him Doc G.

For our interview, Doc G. sat on a folding chair upstairs at Glacier Bay Lodge in the audio-visual room with its big screen in front and a slide projector in the back. I'd been in that room dozens of times while park naturalists gave evening talks.

In the summer of 1966, Doc G. told me, he supervised three Institute of Polar Studies cross-disciplinary scientific teams—geologists, glaciologists, and biologists. He ferried them around the bay in a skiff, from one tent camp to another, making sure that researchers from different disciplines "rubbed elbows" so they'd see what they might otherwise not have noticed within the limits of their own perspective and training.

"I didn't want to be just an administrator and taxi man," Doc G. said, so he measured, "what we began to realize was happening, that the land was slowly moving up." The land was rebounding after the ice melted. Combining information from Bill Field's photographs on the ground and aerial photography based upon methods Bradford Washburn pioneered, Goldthwait created maps to indicate approximate years when the ice had melted in specific areas.

Along with transporting other scientists, Goldthwait took measurements at fifty locations. He worked to determine the high tide line based upon fifteen criteria. He mentioned some of these: the location of a series of beach crests and the plants that grew on them; the presence of plants not tolerant of saltwater; places where the sea had cut into cliffs, since this could only occur in the absence of ice; fossil iceberg marks on beaches; and how waves affected those beaches in present time. He found that the rate of uplift was about three or four centimeters a year near Bartlett Cove, lower at places like Strawberry Island, and higher again at a point across from the Casement Glacier. In the East Arm north of Muir Point, Goldthwait said, it was still too early after the ice receded to get good readings. (The highest rate of current uplift in the bay is in the West Arm across from Reid Inlet at Russell Island, where the land is rising more than 2.8 centimeters per year).

Doc G. also told me this: at the Institute of Polar Studies, glaciologists stored core samples drilled from glaciers located around the world. As it melts, glacial ice releases air that has been trapped in it for thousands of years. When glacial ice is placed in alcohol, the release of air bubbles sounds like bubbles fizzing in champagne.

"In the evening, if you wanted to mix a drink," Doc G. told me at the Lodge in 1979, "you had different choices for ice. You could use ice from a glacier in Peru, or from Greenland, or from the Alps." Doc G. smiled at his joke.

Lonnie Thompson, a paleo-climatologist and former student at the Institute of Polar Studies, realized that the glaciers would melt more quickly as climate change took hold. The information stored in those glaciers—pollen, volcanic dust and ash, the chemistry of sea salt—and, most important, greenhouse gases such as carbon dioxide, nitrous oxide and methane—would be unavailable for the scientific study of climates that existed hundreds and thousands of years ago.

Thompson, who began his field research in 1972, didn't do research in Glacier Bay, although he did study under Doc G. as a graduate student. Thompson now teaches at the School of Earth Sciences at The Ohio State University, where his wife Ellen Mosley-Thompson is director of the Byrd Polar and Climate Research Center. Lonnie Thompson has spent his career retrieving core samples from glaciers around the world, including the Bona-Churchill in Southeast Alaska, before crucial information held in the ice is lost as top layers of ice melt and the glaciers themselves disappear.

In Ohio, Doc G. told me, geologists would relax in the evening drinking gin or bourbon or scotch poured over glacial ice containing ash from extinct volcanoes and dust from atomic tests.

They drank, while water and minerals from ice crystals they studied metabolized into blood and bone.

GRAVEL WATERFALL, UPPER MUIR INLET, 1980

Copyright Fritz Koschmann.

THE CAIRN

There are places that reveal to us aspects of the essence of who we are in relationship to the earth. Any plot of ground can show us this, but some places stand out.

In August 1979, I went to Reid Inlet on a boat chartered by Ross Powell, an Ohio State University geology graduate student doing research for his PhD. We picked up two more geology students camped on a beach in Tarr Inlet. Ross Powell's dissertation advisor was Doc G.

It was Powell's first time hiring a boat in Glacier Bay. As a PhD student, he got little attention in Bartlett Cove at the park headquarters. I wasn't a scientist but I'd been there a few summers, so I offered suggestions, including ideas for boats he might charter. Mostly I suggested fishermen, but they didn't want to stop fishing or to risk their boats in the ice. When Ross found a charter boat, as a thank-you he invited me to come along.

This was Ross Powell's plan: the melt water streams wash out mud and gravel, which sink down to the sea floor. He would analyze the contents of core samples from the sea floor and compare his findings to aerial photos taken by Washburn and to pictures of the advance and retreat of various glaciers recorded by Dr. Field. Excellent photographic records exist about glacial retreat in Glacier Bay, but such history hasn't been tracked in most places. Powell hoped to reconstruct the history of the Glacier Bay glaciers he studied and to use that method to study glaciers that also meet saltwater around the world. Ross Powell grew up in New Zealand and wanted to trace aspects of the glacial history of the Antarctic. In 2013, I read in a *New York Times* article about Ross Powell, professor of sedimentology and climate change at Northern Illinois University, and his Antarctic research.

In Powell's dissertation, the most important outcome of comparing core samples with old glacier positions was that Powell established the first-ever model using sediment records to trace the past history of marine-ending glaciers. It is possible, using this model, to collect cores from areas where the history of past glacier retreat is unknown and determine how fast these glaciers have retreated. This information provides insight, for example, into how such glaciers responded to earlier warming climates thousands of years ago.

Some geologists study glacial ice cores, looking for the particles of dust and pollen deposited in the ice as it formed. Ross Powell took seafloor core samples by letting a steel pipe with a weight and fins on top free-fall from a boat and bore into the seabed. In front of the glaciers, Powell took cores through mud and gravel. (It took a lot of work. If the steel pipe hit rock, they had to move the boat and try again in a different place.)

Reid Glacier was quiet the day we arrived on the boat Ross Powell chartered. In three years, the glacier had changed in major ways. Its face, no longer as steep, sloped back, a sign of inactivity. Much of the ice front was aground, although ice still fell from it. The wind was calm. Saltwater reflected the glacier and icebergs below it, floating as if in a mirror. The glacier, no longer advancing, was stable, retreating slowly. The geologists left for Lamplugh Glacier to take measurements. I rowed to shore near the cabin, then hiked to Reid Glacier.

I wasn't alone on the beach. Near the face of the glacier, I met a photographer who had paddled up the West Arm by kayak and had set up a tent near the cabin. We hiked back to it together. Our paths diverged at the creek that flowed down the hillside near the cabin. He wanted to hike up the streambed and explore the ridge between Lamplugh Glacier and Reid Inlet.

The next day, we invited the photographer out to the boat for dinner. Our skipper was a good cook. The boat floated in circles, at anchor a mile or two from the glacier. We ate peach pie while the photographer told us this story:

"I hiked up the stream behind the Ibachs' cabin and headed toward Lamplugh. Part way between Reid Inlet and Ptarmigan Creek, I saw an old mining cairn." The cairn was probably easy to spot, since the land above Reid Inlet in those years was still mostly bare.

"I knew what it was," the photographer said. "I took apart the pile of stones." A cairn was the traditional way that miners marked their claims.

"An old rusty can was buried underneath. In the can was a scrap of paper. I copied the names, put the paper back in the can, and then I rebuilt the cairn." It would be impossible to find that cairn now, hidden in the alder thickets.

He read us the names in the cairn. The first name was George Shurin, Mike Seiler's brother, and then Shurin's three mining partners. It proved the truth of Shurin's story about mining with Joe Ibach in Reid Inlet.

As if Shurin could have made that up.

KATE BOESSER,
GUSTAVUS, 1995

Courtesy of Kate Boesser.

FRIENDS

The second time my friend Kate was pregnant, she lived on Lemesurier Island for ten days. She left the round house she and her husband built at the four corners in Gustavus, where the road from the dock to Rink Creek crosses the road from the airport to the Park. Her husband took Kate and their daughter across Icy Strait in their boat and rowed them in to the beach. With permission from the current owners, Kate lived in the Ibachs' winter home during the summer of 1984, alone on Lemesurier Island except for her four-year-old daughter and her dog. On Lemesurier, Kate felt calm. She wrote about herself and this difficult pregnancy in the third person: "She was thin, so thin, with a big belly and glacier blue eyes."

At the house, she split wood, built fires, and made rhubarb pies and cakes, weeded the garden, and watched boats pass. On the lawn were berry bushes, white lawn chairs, fruit trees, and a flagpole next to the door.

"In the back room, behind a hanging brown bear skin, we looked at each item in the Ibach 'museum,' old artifacts that included gold pans and mining shovels and picks," Kate told me. "There were old music boxes, photographs, worn knives. I read all of the journals from the time when the Ibachs lived there. We played old LPs on a wind-up phonograph with a big horn on it, and we danced. We walked the beach. We hiked east towards the source of that white rock Muz used to line the pathways. Lemesurier was a magical place."

Kate grew up in Juneau. She is a carver of wood and stone. A woodcut she made, called "The Finest Musician," inspired a book of poems I wrote. Her father was a preacher. Kate was a park naturalist. For six years Kate pointed out the Ibachs' cabin and read from that book of poems to thousands of passengers on the Glacier Bay tour boat and on cruise ships.

"Whenever we got close to Reid Inlet on one of those boats," Kate told me, "I asked the captain to go closer to shore. We would look for the cabin, which was hard to see, and the shed, which was quite visible. I would tell the people on the boat to look for those three Sitka spruces the Ibachs planted and talk about that couple spending summers together in the midst of that vast wilderness. I looked with binoculars for the entrance to one Ibach mine near the water level."

What made the two of us, Kate and me, fall in love with a place and with the story of two people we never knew? Was it the shape of that inlet, the long, almost perfect parabola of shore with a grey-blue glacier at the arc? There was something about the cabin that made the place feel whole: the cabin, the three spruces next to the cabin, and the garden made a place of ice and rock seem warm and welcoming and human.

You looked at the inlet's entrance through the cabin's front door and at the glacier through the back window. The contrast between the cabin and the vast space expressed an essential aspect of being a human being. In that expanse of rock, ice and wind, the scale of the cabin, simple though it was, had a certain kind of elegance. The inlet seemed to hold that rough cabin in an embrace.

A sculpture Kate made in her studio rests now in front of the fireplace in my Portland living room. It is carved in alabaster, and its base is Queen Inlet granite. Kate calls it "Queen Muse."

At the right season and time of day, the light comes into my living room window and shines through that translucent sculpture, and the veins in the rock become the veins of the woman's face.

One thing that leads to loving, whether a best friend or a lover, is that you love, not simply each other, but also something beyond and outside of yourselves. That love might be for other people, for a place, for a dream, an idea, a story, a creation. The two of you hold a set of experiences in common, and you nurture the connection. For Kate and me, at the heart and soul of our connection is a love for Glacier Bay, for Muz and Joe Ibach, for their cabin and the glacier, for Reid Inlet.

DARK ICE AT REID GLACIER, 2011

Copyright Fritz Koschmann.

DESCENDANCY CHART OF JOSEF IBACH

Isidor (Charles) L.[5] Ibach, b. 1834 Leiberstung-Buhl, Baden, d. 1921 Evans, NY
⊨ Mary E.[5] Yenter, b. 1839 Oxford, IA, m. circa 1857 Buffalo, NY, d. 1892 Evans, NY
— George[6] Ibach, b. 1858
— Louise[6] Ibach, b. 1859 North Evans, NY, d. 1859 North Evans, NY
— Charles L.[6] Ibach, b. 1860 North Evans, NY, d. 1934 North Evans, NY
— Lewis[6] Ibach, b. 1861 North Evans, NY, d. 1863 North Evans, NY
— John[6] Ibach, b. 1866 North Evans, NY, d. 1867 North Evans. NY
— Rosa[6] Ibach, b. 1870
— Carolina[6] Ibach, b. 1872
— Albert[6] Ibach, b. 1875
— Joseph P.[6] Ibach, b. 1879 North Evans, NY, d. 1960 Lemesurier Island, AK
  ⊨ Caroline Shirley[6] Sharpe, b. 1885 Ontario, m. 1908 Cordova, Alaska, d. 1959 Juneau, AK
    — Judith[7] Aftergut
    — Kate[7] Boesser

As recorded on ancestry.com by John D. Feagin, Sr.

BECOMING AN IBACH

Spring 1999. Kate was working again for the Park Service as a seasonal naturalist, providing information to summer visitors. She showed me an email she discovered, sent by one of Joe Ibach's relatives to Glacier Bay Lodge and then forwarded to the Park Service. Kate saw the note on a bulletin board.

"Do people there still remember my relatives?" Joe Ibach's great nephew, who lived in Maryland, wanted to know.

"Has anyone responded to it?" I asked Kate.

Her reply was, "I don't think so."

"We should answer it," I told her.

"The Ibach family came from Germany," the nephew, John Feagin, Sr., wrote back to us. "They were not a close family. Joe and his two brothers left New York State for Alaska to escape their father's strict discipline." Joe was the only brother who made it to Alaska as planned. The others turned back.

"As children, we heard stories about them, our 'rich relatives' in Alaska," Feagin wrote. For him, Joe and Muz were the stuff of legend. He said, "They had gold nuggets in the stones of their fireplace."

Kate wrote to Feagin about traveling in the bay as a naturalist for the park. "As a human being on a boat, with towering mountains reaching five-thousand to fourteen-thousand feet above your head," she told him, "in wild weather, with sheer cliffs and bears on the beaches, as a person, you feel smaller and smaller. Then you round a corner and see that tiny red cabin and think about the rhubarb garden, the mine, the glacier calving and those two people, and you feel connected. You're aware of the place on a different scale."

Kate sent stories to Feagin about her Lemesurier Island visits. I sent him Reid Inlet poems. I told Feagin what Ken Youmans said, that Joe Ibach "had everything he wanted."

"Joe and Muz Ibach had no children," Feagin wrote to Kate and me. "They would have liked the two of you. They would have considered you their spiritual children. Therefore, I am going to adopt you into the Ibach family."

He added our names to the Ibach genealogy website he maintains.

"This," he wrote to us, "will confuse the future genealogists."

Feagin listed us as the two children of Joseph P. Ibach, born 1879 in North Evans, New York, and Caroline Shirley Sharpe, born 1885 in Guelph, Ontario, Canada. Caroline Sharpe married Joe Ibach in 1908. Joe Ibach was born in 1879, the same year that John Muir saw briefly in fog the great glacier that filled the bay's East Arm.

Feagin sent us adoption certificates, signed by Muz and Joe Ibach. Feagin has a sense of humor.

Kate wrote to John: "Since I am now part of your family, I want you to know I've been told that I am a direct descendent of Anne Hutchinson, who was tried, convicted and banished from the Massachusetts Bay Colony in 1637." An educated woman and a midwife as well as the mother of fifteen or more children (the numbers in the sources vary), Hutchinson led discussions focused on the idea that a personal connection, "an intuition of spirit," rather than good works or paying attention to the Bible and church elders, would lead to being chosen by God. Hutchinson's beliefs created a division with the Puritan clergy. In a second trial, this time by the Church, Hutchinson was excommunicated.

Feagin replied, "Strangely enough, it was my ancestors on my mother's side, the Maltbies, who helped persecute Anne Hutchinson. The Maltbies married into the Ibach family. My eighth great-grandfather, Rev. William Bartholomew, was one of forty-nine members of the clergy who took an active part in Anne Hutchinson's trial and subsequent persecution." As a Mormon, John Feagin, Sr., was interested in genealogy.

From Massachusetts, Anne Hutchinson moved to Rhode Island and then to the Dutch colony in New York. A river in the Bronx bears her name. She was an ancestor of President Franklin D. Roosevelt and of both presidents Bush. On her father's side, Hutchinson was descended from Charlemagne and Alfred the Great; on her mother's side from Edward I of England and his ancestors Henry II of England and Eleanor of Aquitaine. Two hundred and eighty-five years after her trial, a monument was dedicated near the State House in Boston honoring her as a "courageous exponent of civil liberty and religious toleration."

John sent Kate an apology: "For what our ancestor did to yours, from my whole family lineage, I ask forgiveness from you and all of your family on their behalf. ... It has now fallen upon me as a descendent," Feagin wrote, "to truly ask forgiveness for what they did. Please forgive my grandfathers for what they did to your ancestor. Anne Hutchinson was a person of courage and faith. She dared to speak directly with God and to obtain personal revelations, and she was right."

He signed the letter, "Your cousin John."

"To be embraced three hundred years later by the family that persecuted my ancestor and ultimately caused her death is incredible," Kate replied. "Thank you for the gift of kinship."

I suppose this makes Kate and me sisters. In any case, we are sisters in spirit, and we care about the same things—about healing family stories through art, about community, and about Glacier Bay. The adoption surprised us, but perhaps Feagin recognized that Kate and I had already adopted Muz and Joe Ibach.

And so, through John and Kate, I, too, became linked to an early Puritan history from which, as the daughter of first- and second-generation Jewish immigrants, I felt a subtle sense of separation. Through Feagin's actions, the people I come from, survivors of the long arc of Jewish history, are linked to Puritans and to Mormons as well as to the victim and perpetrators in Anne Hutchinson's trials. My connection to them is imagined, but perhaps most connections are.

Would it occur to most people to send this apology for an ancestor's actions? Maybe, but I am not certain. I don't believe that current generations are responsible for what their ancestors did. Nonetheless, I do believe we should be aware and do what we can to restore the balance. John Feagin had declared that Kate was now included in his family, so his relationship to Anne Hutchinson's descendant was close, not distant. Still, it takes a big person to relate to history personally. In a similar situation, I hope that I, too, would ask for forgiveness, as the United States finally did years after the imprisonment of U.S. citizens of Japanese extraction in World War II internment camps, as South Africans did after Apartheid.

John Feagin, Sr. sent me one more note, before I lost track of him. The package contained an original letter written, after Muz Ibach died, on fragile and yellowing paper in Joe Ibach's spidery hand. The date is June 1, 1959.

It said: "Muz is resting beneath the cottonwoods where she wished to be."

Was "spiritual children" an Ibach phrase? That idea, applied to Kate and me, may have been John Feagin's own or part of his Mormon faith. Still, the idea seems consistent with what I knew of Joe and Muz Ibach, who treated George Shurin's half-brother Mike Seiler like an adopted son.

I think Feagin's request for forgiveness is profound, even if human identities are transient as phosphorescence that glows in a sailboat's wake in the moonlight.

REID INLET RETURN

In the summer of 2004, Kate wrote this to me from Gustavus: "The glaciers are wasting away in a year of unusual warmth. You should come to see them. You won't recognize them."

I didn't go north that summer. I didn't want to see the change. I knew that the glaciers were melting, of course, but I couldn't quite accept that the familiar shapes of glaciers I knew were changing to that extent.

Kate told me, "When we moved to Gustavus from Juneau and built the house in 1977 and '78, we had next door neighbors who had lived in Gustavus a long time. They said they didn't go up Glacier Bay any more. 'The bay has changed so much,' one neighbor said, 'that we can't bear to see it.'" I knew how those neighbors felt.

But the next summer, Kate and I returned to Reid Inlet. We paddled Kate's double kayak from the tour boat drop-off point at Queen Inlet. Past Composite Island, we crossed the West Arm from east to west, not in rain, but in sunshine and flat calm water. (Picture t-shirts and sun cream).

The tide was beginning to ebb by the time we reached the west side, so we paddled along the shore. When the tide flows out past a point of land, water inside the point near the shoreline circles back in the opposite direction. Hugging the shore, we found it easier to paddle in that back eddy, where the water flowed north as the main force of the tide went south. (I knew this strategy from my Bainbridge Island racing days on a 26-foot sailboat that its captain named the *Old Crow*. The skipper of the *Old Crow* was Norwegian, and he had sailed since his childhood in Norway. He could climb the mast sailing alone if a sail snagged or a line got hung up. He could set the spinnaker by himself. There was always a bottle of Old Crow in the galley hanging over a hook from a piece of thin line tied around the bottle's neck. We drank Old Crow on that boat the *Old Crow* in cold weather to warm us up and in hot weather to cool down. We won Bainbridge Island races by sneaking along the beach in the quiet back eddy while the big boats, the forty- and fifty-footers, sailed mid-channel and flailed against the wind and tide.)

FLOWERS AT REID INLET: *DRYAS* AND INDIAN PAINTBRUSH, WATERCOLOR, 2012
Copyright Carole Baker.

Kate and I pulled the kayak up the beach in Reid Inlet and unloaded our gear. In 2005, the cabin was still standing, minus much of its roof. In *Glacier Bay: The Land and the Silence*, published in the late 1960s, Dave Bohn imagined that the Ibachs' cabin, already leaning, might continue to stand for another twenty years, but that cabin was still upright. Above the cabin, it was now almost impossible to hike in the hills that had once been bare gravel. The cabin was nearly surrounded by alders that created an almost impenetrable forest, their branches growing low along the ground. One alder trunk held the cabin up. The three spruce trees the Ibachs planted had grown tall and shaded the garden site completely. Their rhubarb, a sun-loving species, was nowhere to be found.

In the years since the Ibachs spent summers in Reid Inlet, the land, once pressed down by ice, had rebounded. The Ibachs' pothole was completely dry, and saltwater no longer reached it. Kate and I stood on its edge and gazed at a garden of *Dryas drummondii* and Indian paintbrush.

Dryas drummondii is a low plant that grows in circles. Its common name is mountain avens. It is one of the first plants to grow in deglaciated land after ice recedes. The plants take root in gravel and grow in the absence of soil. A *Dryas* plant expands, radiating out. In time, the neighboring plants touch each other and cover the land in a continuous mat. Growing in gravel, *Dryas* in seed seems to visually soften the landscape. That day in Reid Inlet, sunlight filtered through open seedpods before the seeds blew away, resembling how sunlight glows through the silver strands of an old woman's hair.

We pitched our tent in gravel near the pothole. I watched the light fade through the tent's front opening. That night we slept under stars. Waking up in morning stillness, from inside the tent as the sun rose, I saw shadows flit across the roof of the tent and heard the wing beats of a flock of tiny birds.

That day, under clouds and then showers, we walked from the cabin to Reid Glacier, three miles. Only one part of Reid Glacier's face still met the incoming tide. A stream flowing out from beneath the ice undulated through the gravel, and a line of icebergs floated in it. Freshwater merged with saltwater, changing the sea's color at the head of Reid Inlet from blue to pale milky grey-green.

We walked across the gravel bar on the north side of the ice face and stepped into an indentation in the ice. Reid Glacier had temporarily created a tiny, perfect meditation space. We stood there in silence, one after the other, and drank drops of the ice as it melted so the ice became part of us.

Back at the spit that evening, I inspected battalions of *Dryas* in seed. *Dryas drummondii* seeds drift in the wind the way that dandelion seeds do.

"Look, Kate." I pointed, and Kate, too, bent down. The closed *Dryas* seedpods formed a twisted cluster. A dandelion seed resembles a miniature, inverted umbrella; the tops of the *Dryas* seeds looked more like feathers. At the end of each seed's stem, I noticed a point, like the tip of a tiny arrow. At our feet, feathered seed stalks stood straight upright, stuck between pieces of gravel so that winds from the glacier could not dislodge them. The tops of those seeds waved in the wind like the banners of a miniature army.

The second night came the deluge, and our tent's rain fly leaked. I was using Kate's husband's sleeping bag. It was long enough that I could curl up with dry clothes in the top when the bottom of the sleeping bag got soaked in a downhill puddle near the door of the tent.

The next morning we carried the kayaks to the water and paddled, hugging the shore to stay away from cruise ships moving through the main channel. Rain poured down from clouds so low that we couldn't see the hills on the other side of the West Arm. We might be able to hear a ship's motor, but we wouldn't know where it was. We heard thunder and saw lightning. Rain hit the surface of the water hard enough that the drops of water bounced up.

We followed the shore of the Gilbert Peninsula, called Gilbert Island on the old maps. With the land rising three centimeters a year, the tides don't come up on the shore as far as they once did. The Gilbert Peninsula was now an island only at extremely high tides. Along the peninsula's steep rock shores, we passed waterfalls roaring down. On the rock face we saw specks of magenta, dwarf fireweed in bloom, with grey and green all around.

It is easier to pay attention to a place when you are moving at human speed, paddling with the rain pouring over you, working hard to keep yourself dry in a world of mist and fog. It is true that my hands got cold and rain slid down my wrists from my gloves. It might seem that I would be suffering, but it wasn't like that at all. There is joy in situations where one-pointed attention is required, like sailing, like writing, like paddling in rainy weather in a place where it can be dangerous. On that day when the elements conspired, while fog and rain surrounded the kayak, we moved slowly through cold water, listening to our breathing and the sound of the paddles. I had the experience, not simply of joy, but more. It was ecstasy.

We arrived at Blue Mouse Cove soaking wet with half an hour before the tour boat arrived—enough time, alone on the beach, to strip off our clothes, soaked from sweat under rain gear, and put on our last dry clothes. It was still drizzling, but there was a kind of joy in exposing our bare skin to the air.

If, as I've heard, when I'm dying, the highlights of life will flash before my eyes, then I think as I lie down to die, I'll see waterfalls and dwarf fireweed on the hillsides padding with Kate south of Reid Inlet in the rain.

MIKE SEILER (LEFT), VIOLA THE CAMP COOK (CENTER), AND LES PARKER,
LEROY MINE, PTARMIGAN CREEK, CIRCA 1942
Courtesy of Gustavus Historical Archives and Antiquities.

LESLIE PARKER

"Do you think Joe Ibach was satisfied?" I once asked Gustavus homesteader Leslie Parker. He was in his 70s, the age I am now. Les Parker had owned the Leroy gold mine at Ptarmigan Creek, around the point and just north of the Ibachs' place at Reid Inlet. He and I sat at the kitchen table in the Gustavus house he had built on land he homesteaded, next to the road near the Salmon River. He had come with his family to Gustavus in 1917.

Les Parker slowly shook his head, looking down at his cup of coffee. I didn't drink coffee in those days, especially not the instant coffee he served. When I visited Les and Bonnie Parker, I picked wild yarrow in their yard, steeped the feathery leaves in hot water, and added honey for tea. Les Parker died in 1997 at the age of ninety-three. The land next to the site of his house is now the Gustavus cemetery.

Les Parker didn't think Joe Ibach was satisfied. I didn't ask Parker for reasons. Why didn't I ask? I think that the answer no longer mattered to me. I hadn't known anyone who was satisfied, so the idea, when I first heard it, that Joe Ibach had everything he wanted, surprised me. Looking back, I wasn't seeking the truth about whether Muz and Joe Ibach had been satisfied with their lives. I was fairly sure they were. I was looking for the idea that one could be satisfied. I was looking for the question.

I needed the idea that someone, anyone, could have everything they wanted, because this idea had seemed impossible. But if the Ibachs could, then so could I. Once I knew that I could have everything I wanted, I might be willing to know what I wanted and admit to myself that I knew it.

IBACH CABIN CRADLED BY ALDERS, REID INLET, 2007
Copyright Kate Boesser.

WHAT SHE WANTED

What did she want, that young woman I was once? What was she asking for? It is said that when a woman leaves home, it's because there is something she's seeking. Did she want money, fame and recognition? If she did, that was long ago.

Did she truly want everything? What was the "everything" she wanted? She probably didn't want more possessions in those years when she often felt overwhelmed walking into a department store. To want it all sounded like greed. It sounded like endless desire. She thought, all those years ago, young and confused, that she should want what she was supposed to want, like marriage or money or children. She had thought that wanting what she herself wanted wasn't allowed.

She had made up her mind that it was dangerous to want, when she was young, a child. She wasn't punished often, because she decided at an early age to be good, or look like she was. She watched her younger brother being punished after he set the kitchen curtains on fire and smoked cigarettes as a boy. It seemed to her that his punishment came from wanting too much and reaching a bit too far.

She might be willing to let herself know what she wanted if she thought it was possible to have it, but that, too, didn't seem to be allowed. She wanted to have a bat mitzvah ceremony, but she wasn't allowed to write a speech. She forgot that she wanted anything, wanted less, forgot to ask. It seemed dangerous to have ideas that were hers. She did what she was told, got straight As, but decided that all of her wanting would only be for that which she couldn't have.

She said she wanted to finish a book, and then she would marry and have children. That was a clever plan! She took forty years to write it! She had made a decision to never get married when she was five years old, and then she forgot that she'd made it. She didn't even know what she didn't want, back then. She didn't truly want to get married, although she was married for a couple of years. What she doesn't want is clearer now.

She wanted a father who wasn't in a wheelchair, a father who didn't shout. She wanted a mother whose mind was clear, although it was hard to imagine. She couldn't have everything she wanted unless, as she came to see, she could choose her mother and father exactly the way they were. Her parents simply were that way. Even if she didn't realize it then, they had given her what she needed.

Little did she know that many years later she would dream of her father the night before his death. In the dream, at least for a moment, all her anger with him disappeared. She felt peaceful, too, a few weeks before her mother died, after they finally fell in love with each other.

All along, she did want to write this book. She met writers of other books about Glacier Bay early on. She felt jealous of some of them at first, until she came to see that no one could write the same book because no one else was living her life.

To be honest, she never needed much, this child of a father who knew poverty and was thrilled to spend money on her; this child of a mother who thought that, no matter how much money they had, they would never have enough, and that soon all the money would be gone. But her mother paid for dance and piano lessons before it occurred to the daughter to want them. The daughter was a child who knew from her own life how many situations money could not solve.

She wanted to live true to herself, not adapting to other people's desires. That took a long time to discover: the difference between fulfilling desires in a way congruent with integrity and having love affairs with guilt in their wake. She wanted to know people deeply, to hear their wisdom and to find nourishment for her soul and theirs. Most of the things she wanted, like knowing how to trust herself, like being known and loved profoundly, like being honored and honoring herself, she recognized later as important and real, even if they were intangible, and unreachable for too long. She wanted to forgive others and herself, to be accepted for who she was. She wanted to find her own direction in life the way she felt the unseen path with her feet when she walked in the woods in the dark.

From Glacier Bay and its people she learned to live simply. She wanted to experience the mystic, that sense of oneness and ecstasy. For her that sense still comes from clear light and air, from talking with good friends, from playing music, from dance, from sexuality, and from learning of scientific discoveries, like the fact that halibut are territorial and that the DNA of the brown bears in upper Glacier Bay is different from that of neighboring populations because the bears were separate, in Glacier Bay, from other bears during the Little Ice Age. There exist in the world countless points of access to the beautiful and the ecstatic. From the time she set foot in the gravel there, for her, Glacier Bay was one of those places.

In her thirties she thought that the way to have everything she wanted might be to not want very much. At age seventy, she knows that to live simply is an access to joy, and that not wanting too many things is different from settling for less.

Now she knows she can live a fulfilled life if she honors herself, other people and the earth, if she works to make the best choices and connects with the mystery of it all. She knows she can live this way anywhere if she's willing to remain present to a sense of wonder. She can bring her joy to a clear cut on the Oregon coast if she lets herself feel her grief in the midst of the slash and the mud. She knows the contradiction of feeling wonder and grief in the presence of the thousand-year-old hemlock stumps in Glacier Bay. Those trees, buried in gravel, cut down by ice, were revealed when rivers from the melting glaciers washed the gravels away. To her, the remains of those old trees seemed like pure revelation.

Of course, it is true that everyone connected with Glacier Bay does not experience ecstasy and joy. For some people, the access points to joy and fulfillment come through marriage and children and work. For her they also come from dancing and singing, through gentle touch, by putting her hands in the dirt, by making peace with and forgiving mistakes, in beautiful and deep conversations, by looking for the highest and best actions to take in any situation she faces. Now that she has many years-long friendships and enough money to live a simple life, there isn't much else she wants, except fulfilling her purpose for being born on this earth, even if she never knows what it is.

Will this current joy be a brief memory? Will she experience ecstasy at the moment of death? Is it okay to want to live in ecstasy and joy on an earth filled with people's pain?

Is it possible for her to have everything she wants? The answer to that question is yes, as long as she accepts that everything in life changes and that many things can't be changed by her; as long as she remembers that life exists in each moment and that things in each particular moment exist the way they are. Reid Glacier won't stop retreating. People and glaciers do what they do. But if she can have any influence, she wants change to occur in the best possible direction, since it's clear to her now that human action and intention shape the world in powerful ways.

She happened to come to Glacier Bay. It helped to wake her up. She could stand on the beach at Bartlett Cove and focus her eyes close by or in the distance. She could focus far away at Point Carolus across Icy Strait or on bear tracks near her feet; she could focus on rye grass, beach greens and kelp, and waves that lapped at the shore; or look at snow on the Fairweather peaks one hundred miles away. It was hard to make a choice about where to look, because all of it to her seemed exquisite, even low tide and the muck. Each slight move of her eyes changed her vision's frame. The challenge of choosing where to focus seemed to open up her brain.

That beauty and requirement to pay attention, the presence of danger—bears, hypothermia and rain—all of this helped her to be more alert than she was in the city, to be present to the lichens, the eagles, the salmonberries, as well as to people who waved on the road, said hello, and who laughed at her foibles and their own.

Today she wants a few possessions, a little more than enough money, and a home. She wants to be part of more than one community of friends. A simple life might not be what everyone wants, but for her, it is sufficient. She once wanted the basics required to live a writer's contemplative life. She wanted to be at peace, the kind of peace that her bipolar mother longed for. Now that she is older—rounding third base, as a friend of hers says—she thinks that the capacity for ecstasy is what she saw in the photograph of Muz and Joe: that they pasted those photos on the wall in the cabin, of deserts and mansions and clothes from Montgomery Ward, because the two of them were clear about what they didn't need. All those years ago she kept looking for a place to be happy. Now she knows happiness is created within. It is not based upon geography, although being rooted in a place can help. She thinks that Muz and Joe Ibach were in touch with the source of their joy.

Some days now she wakes up into clouds and the rain and fog of autumn, the wind blowing fir branches down, and she feels, not a stab, but a long deep pain in her heart for what is no longer—for first love; childhood drives in the Ozarks; and the boom and crack that Reid Glacier made in the days when its whole ice front still flowed to saltwater. She feels a sense of pain in her heart that she knows is more than her own—the pain of what's disappearing, a pain felt by all of us, if we don't turn away—the pain and loss of the world.

It seemed to her that Muz and Joe Ibach were living a joy-filled life, but who knows. She also thinks that Muz might have lived on if Joe had died first. After all, Mike Seiler said that Muz was the stronger one. Seiler probably meant that Muz had the emotional and spiritual strength that comes from facing your own challenges straight, the kind of strength worth having. And there's no doubt that the Ibachs felt pain, the pain that everyone has.

She didn't know pain then the way she does now, although often she wakes up in gratitude for the beauty of the world, for the people she knows, and for having lived long enough, as the Hebrew prayer says, to come to this happy time. Some mornings she wakes up with pain in her heart for what's missing, what's lost and what's gone. She didn't know the Ibachs' inner lives: their sadness, disappointments, lost chances. She doesn't know what it's like to live with one person for many years and how it feels when that person dies. Still, she saw, in the eyes of two people photographed standing on that Lemesurier Island porch, what she thought was missing within her.

Forty years after she first read about Muz and Joe Ibach, she can simply say, for the moment, that she has everything she wants, although that changes with time. For her, the next question is, what does she now want for others, beyond her self, that she can help provide?

114 Now that she has everything she wants, she wants to give people joy. That's what she can see so far. She wonders what it will take for us all to evolve, to find perspectives and a new story to live from, as a response to climate and other challenges in the world; to be a species that looks after other people, the air, water, and land that give us life; to treat everything with reverence; to be as aware as we can of our impacts; and tread lightly because we know that everything is interconnected.

FOG

September 2008. 6 a.m. I am floating in the waters of Reid Inlet again, on board a catamaran that sleeps eight, the boat that Kate's husband Fritz built by hand in his shop next to their house in Gustavus over a period of ten winters. The boat's name is the *Great Sea*. It is forty feet long and twenty feet wide.

I wake up. It is early morning, and I look out of the cabin window. We circle at anchor. The glacier is barely visible in fog.

Last night Ken Youmans' daughter Aimee stood with us on the deck. She told us stories of Reid Inlet. When she was a child, Aimee visited the Ibachs with her father. She remembers the cabin and prospecting with her dad when she was seven or eight years old. She walked up the creek bed behind the cabin as her father staked claims on the ridge between Reid Inlet and Ptarmigan Creek. She remembers Muz Ibach's flowers. This year Aimee is sixty years old.

"I wonder what it will be like when this place is covered with forests and looks like the rest of Southeast Alaska," someone said to Aimee as a child. Her incredulous answer, at age seven, was: "That will never happen here!" Kate and I hear the question and her answer and look around us at the ice face that slopes back. It has swaths of gravel and rock on each side. The glacier is disappearing.

In the morning, I look out through a porthole as the fog begins to lift. The sun moves higher. As the light increases, I'm aware that we are not living in a fairy tale enveloped in mist.

We float in water the color of pale turquoise near gray hills. The water of Reid Inlet, flat calm, reveals a reflection of the creek that flows down the outwash fan near the Ibach cabin site. The inlet mirrors the cottonwoods with yellowing leaves growing on the spit. I can see the three dark spruce trees the Ibachs planted, and alders where the cabin is hidden. Remains of the fog float along the ridgeline and halfway down the mountainsides across the inlet.

Fritz pulls the anchor, starts the motor, and we leave with the morning tide. I hold this picture of Reid Glacier in the early morning fog in my mind when I return home

THE *GREAT SEA* IN FOG, 2006

Copyright Carole Baker.

to Portland a few days later. I awaken and sleep while centuries-old ice is turning into water again.

It takes time to get to know a place and its glaciers, its mountains, its shape; others know Glacier Bay better than I. But no one can discount the fact that while we are listening and learning to know it, in the meantime, everything changes. There always remains the mystery, and knowing what we can know takes time.

No one can notice all of these changes as they happen minute by minute. A species with that ability would be unable to act. We often don't live aware that we are part of the change and that we contribute to it. Every now and then we might notice the grief about change that exists below the surface of our awareness. The ground we hope is solid is shifting and changing beneath our feet.

We don't deserve happiness, my Portland rabbi once said in a talk he gave. Our life is not about what we deserve or what we don't deserve. Every life has its pain. Life is given to us as a gift, said the rabbi. Our job is to nourish the soul. Our task, because we are given a soul, is to keep an inner light alive. How do we each nourish the soul? That depends upon each of us. In my case, curiosity, prayer and wonder; through loving whom and what I love; through writing, dance and singing; every now and then, by standing up for what I believe. All I can do is choose the best path I can see, or recover and make amends when I choose poorly. How I nurture my soul is my story. Then I will die, and my body will break down into the earth and minerals it came from.

"Most people assume that the wilderness experience is an aesthetic problem, that is, a spiritual one," Chuck Jurasz once told me when he spent summers in Glacier Bay researching whales. "People talk about refreshing the spirit. You know, the heavy breathers are trying to protect the environment, as if the issue is emotional," he said. "It's a semantics problem. What they're really talking about is brainwashing, but it's not a negative connotation. You wash your mind. It's clean."

I think scientist Chuck Jurasz and my rabbi were talking about the same thing in slightly different languages. Chuck Jurasz agrees.

ENTRANCE TO REID INLET, FEBRUARY 1968
Copyright Dave Bohn.

"Take care," Kate signs her emails to me, and the meanings harmonize. "Take care" as in "take care of yourself." "Take care" as in "be careful." "Take care" as in "pay attention, be focused in the moment, and be present." To take care means to care for what I love: both places and people, as the Ibachs did. The meanings of the phrase "take care" hold together, they resonate and build upon each other. "Take care:" Is that what this place would say, if it could speak?

The Ibachs are gone. The glacier will be gone. We will all be gone, in time. The Reid Inlet spit rises higher as it rebounds from the weight of thousands of feet of ice. Reid Glacier formed when water froze and fell in layers as snow. For this moment the glacier is still alive. It will melt, and my body will melt. The landscape will dissolve.

Reid Glacier, retreating, shrinking, for a moment lies silent beneath the clouds.

REID GLACIER AND
DRYAS FIELD, 2004
Copyright Sean Neilson.

AFTERWORD

This book, the first in a sequence, follows a particular thread. The books that follow have related themes. All of them, from my perspective, express the idea of honoring.

To honor has a number of aspects: to celebrate, appreciate, acknowledge, respect and accept and to simply be present. This first book focuses mostly on celebration, appreciation and acknowledgement: it is possible to celebrate the glaciers, even if they're being lost; to appreciate the Ibachs, although they have been dead for fifty years; and to acknowledge our own part individually and as a species in the alterations we call climate change.

"You can't teach honoring," my editor Megan once told me. "You can only tell stories about it." If she's right, and I think she is, then what I mean by honoring may not make a difference for you. Where and from whom did you learn to honor? Whom, what and how do you honor now? That is more important.

What matters, I think, is how we live, and so I will tell you this: to honor, for me, is to make the best choices I can see in any situation, no matter how challenging. To honor includes reverence. I began to learn the first requirement for honoring on a daily basis in Glacier Bay. It is to trust myself.

The attempt to honor whatever I face has offered a path to follow in unknown territory. Making the best choice I can see allows for an experience of inner peace while responding to the world "outside."

In a process that began as the Little Ice Age ended, Reid Glacier and others are melting. Human activities speed that process up.

This series of books is one response when I think of changes in the world and I wonder, "How do I honor this?"

Judith Aftergut
Portland, OR
July 8, 2015

ACKNOWLEDGEMENTS

It is usual to say in book acknowledgements: "There are more people than I ever could thank." All of you who supported and contributed to this writing over a period of forty years have helped me to learn to see for myself and to learn how to choose the best path. In your presence I have experienced being profoundly known, accepted and loved, including, finally, by myself. It is my greatest wish to have returned this favor to you and others.

Glacier Bay and its people inspired me, and many people kept me writing: Dave Bohn, Chuck Jurasz and Greg Streveler, who saw potential early on. They offered faith when I didn't have it, along with mentoring and periodic input. Megan Brown helped me learn to trust my own judgment. Kate Boesser read multiple versions of this book and shared the interviews in rough form with thousands of cruise ship and tour boat passengers. Barry Schieber insisted in the gentlest way that something I wrote should be published.

A series of writing teachers, editors and colleagues gave me courage and also stuck to their guns: Carol Bly, Kim Stafford, Dave Bohn, Meriwether Falk, Caroline Taylor, Bert Speelpenning, Kathy Hocker, and Brenna McLaughlin. A series of reviewers read some or all of it: Rick Grandjean, Carol Kanter and David Markewitz, among others. I would not have completed this writing without the members of the Gustavus writers group—Abigail Calkin, Fran Kelso and Kate Boesser, as well as Sally Lesh and Rita Wilson, both of blessed memory, as we say in Judaism. At our weekly meetings, they provided exquisite feedback, helped check facts, and offered examples of fine writing along with many humorous and practical stories and suggestions. Cathy Drown, Sarah Eichorn, Lynn Marie Jackson, Bob Jackson, Walter Collins and Barbara Coffman, Phoenisis McEachin, Ron McComb, Rena Davis and Tony Illo helped to heal my body and spirit. I thank Ruth Shields, who listened as I read the manuscript out loud while she drove cross-country. Leia Reedijk created a beautiful design.

The town of Gustavus could compete for percentage of librarians per capita with any place on earth. I thank you all: Lynne Jensen, Carolyn Elder, Artemis Bona Dea,

ACKNOWLEDGEMENTS

Kate Boesser and Rusty Yerxa; and *merci beaucoup* to their inspiration and mentor, Doris Howe.

I thank Dave Bohn for his book *Glacier Bay: The Land and the Silence* and for the photographs I am honored to include. I thank each of the photographers for their work and the benefits of their vision: Bradford Washburn, Bruce Black, Bob Howe, Fritz Koschmann, and Sean Neilson. Thanks to Tony Decaneas of the Decaneas Archive, who made Washburn's photograph available, and to Aimee Youmans for first showing me Bruce Black's photograph of Joe Ibach and Ken Youmans. I thank Carole Baker for her glorious paintings. I am indebted to Linda and Lee Parker of Gustavus Historical Archives and Antiquities for their hard work and great website. I thank George and Lynne Jensen, Ted Hoppin, Anne Sommer, John and Linda Galvin, and everyone who gave me a place to stay and fed me dinner in their house, their cabin or their trailer in Gustavus, on Bainbridge Island, and in Portland.

I am extraordinarily grateful to this place, to the National Park Service, and to everyone who supported this quest. I thank a series of former superintendents—Bob Howe, Tom Ritter, Mike Tollefson and John Chapman—as well as the people I have quoted and interviewed: Dave Bohn, Greg Streveler, Carolyn Elder, Chuck Jurasz, Ken Youmans, Nell Parker, Aimee Youmans, Carol Janda, Archie Chase, Mike Seiler, George Shurin, Les Parker and Fred Howe. (I collected Les Parker's stories, although he never agreed to be taped.) I thank John Feagin, Sr.

I acknowledge and appreciate the work of Landmark Worldwide, its staff, and the worldwide community of friends I am privileged to be part of through these programs, including Joey Marguerite, Sharon Jones, Chris Jones, Deborah London Baker, Leah Henderson, and Vickie Peck.

I am immensely grateful to Megan Brown, who saw my way of viewing the world, reflected it back, supported expanding it, and shared her own; to Kate Boesser, who responded to every request and stood for this book when I wanted to give up; and to

Greg Streveler, whose knowledge, awareness and love of this place continually inspired me to care about it. Any mistakes and omissions are my own.

I am grateful to my parents and my family for their love and their enormous gifts—from my mother's lineage, intuition and strength, and from my father's, generosity. Without their love and support, this project could not have been fulfilled. I especially thank my brother Dennis for his wisdom and authenticity.

All of you have helped to save me. May you all be blessed!

REFERENCES

Bohn, Dave. *Glacier Bay: The Land and the Silence.* San Francisco: Sierra Club, 1967.

Fagan, Brian M. *The Little Ice Age: How Climate Made History 1300–1850.* New York, NY: Basic Books, 2000.

Feagin, John, Sr. "Descendancy Chart of Josef Ibach." RootsWeb. http://homepages.rootsweb.ancestry.com/~ibach/josefibach2.htm.

Fox, Douglas. "Scientists Drill through 2,400 Feet of Antarctic Ice for Climate Clues." *Scientific American*, January 16, 2015. http://www.scientificamerican.com/article/scientists-drill-through-2-400-feet-of-antarctic-ice-for-climate-clues/.

Gorman, James. "Deep Under Antarctica, Looking for Signs of Life." *The New York Times,* January 14, 2013.

Heacox, Kim. *The Only Kayak: A Journey Into the Heart of Alaska.* Guilford, CT: Lyons Press, 2005.

Lentfer, Hank. *Faith of Cranes: Finding Hope and Family in Alaska.* Seattle, WA: The Mountaineers Books, 2011.

Parker, Geoffrey. "Lessons From the Little Ice Age." *The New York Times*, March 22, 2014.

The Parks on the Air Book

225 Main Street, Newington, CT 06111-1400 USA
www.arrl.org

Copyright © 2023 by

The American Radio Relay League, Inc.

*Copyright secured under the
Pan-American Convention*

All rights reserved. No part of this work may be reproduced in any form except by written permission of the publisher. All rights of translation are reserved.

Printed in the USA

Quedan reservados todos los derechos

ISBN: 978-1-62595-174-8

First Edition

About the Cover Photos

ARRL member Michael Martens, KB9VBR, of Wausau, Wisconsin, produces the YouTube channel "KB9VBR Antennas" (**youtube.com/@KB9VBRAntennas**). The photograph was taken at the Dells of Eau Claire county park in Marathon County, WI. The Ice Age National Scenic Trail, K-4238, runs through the park.

ARRL member Jherica Goodgame, KI5HTA, of Avon, Connecticut has served as a summer intern at ARRL Headquarters. She attends college at the University of Mississippi and participates in POTA. The photograph was taken at the John W. Kyle State Park, K-2540, in Sardis, MS.